W9-BXH-028

Chicago Public Library
Avalon Branch
8148 S. Stony Island Ave.
Chicago, IL 60617

A Teen's Guide to

Creating
WEB PAGES
and
BLOGS

Chicago Public Library
Avalon Branch
8148 S. Stony Island Ave.
Chicago, IL 60617

A Teen's Guide to

Creating
WEB PAGES
and
BLOGS

Benjamin Selfridge, Peter Selfridge, and Jennifer Osburn

PRUFROCK PRESS INC.
WACO, TEXAS

Chicago Public Library
Avalon Branch
8148 S. Stony Island Ave.
Chicago, IL 60617

Library of Congress Cataloging-in-Publication Data

Selfridge, Benjamin.
 A teen's guide to creating web pages and blogs / Benjamin Selfridge, Peter Selfridge, and Jennifer Osburn.
   p. cm.
 Previously published under title: Kid's guide to creating web pages for home and school, 2004.
 Includes bibliographical references.
 ISBN-13: 978-1-59363-345-5 (pbk.)
 ISBN-10: 1-59363-345-9 (pbk.)
 1. Web sites—Design—Amateurs' manuals. 2. Blogs—Design—Amateurs' manuals. 3. Internet and teenagers. I.
Selfridge, Peter. II. Osburn, Jennifer, 1983– III. Selfridge, Benjamin. Kid's guide to creating web pages for home and
school. IV. Title.
 TK5105.888.S454 2009
 006.7--dc22
                      2008040044

Copyright ©2009 Prufrock Press Inc.

Edited by Lacy Compton
Production Design by Marjorie Parker

ISBN-13: 978-1-59363-345-5
ISBN-10: 1-59363-345-9

The purchase of this book entitles the buyer to reproduce student activity pages for classroom use only. Other use
requires written permission of publisher. All rights reserved.

At the time of this book's publication, all facts and figures cited are the most current available; all telephone numbers,
addresses, and Web site URLs are accurate and active; all publications, organizations, Web sites, and other resources
exist as described in this book; and all have been verified. The authors and Prufrock Press make no warranty or
guarantee concerning the information and materials given out by organizations or content found at Web sites, and
we are not responsible for any changes that occur after this book's publication. If you find an error or believe that
a resource listed here is not as described, please contact Prufrock Press.

Prufrock Press Inc.
P.O. Box 8813
Waco, TX 76714-8813
Phone: (800) 998-2208
Fax: (800) 240-0333
http://www.prufrock.com

R0421830448

Contents

About This Book

THERE are lots of things to learn about computers and the Internet, and lots of ways of learning them. Because HTML is the basic technology underlying Web pages, there are plenty of HTML resources out there, including books on HTML for different skill levels, online tutorials for kids, and courses at school, your local community college, and perhaps even your library. So, why did we write this book?

There are a couple of reasons. First, most of the books and other resources seem to us to be too advanced and too complicated for what teens want to do on the Web. Some are essentially reference books, and others assume the reader is already comfortable with using a computer in a technical way. Second (and this is related to the first reason), we wanted a book for teens. We wanted to provide information for those of you who have grown up with computers, computer games, and the Internet but may never have really explored computer technology. Of course, advanced technology can be mastered only through years of study, but we believe there is no reason why any motivated child, teen, or adult cannot learn some straightforward technologies, like HTML.

By the way, because this book is written by three of us, we usually use "we" in the text. But sometimes Ben takes over and mentions something from his point of view (usually to his dad's detriment). At other times, when sharing her expertise, Jennifer takes over. In both of those instances, the text switches to "I."

So, how should you use this book? The answer is very easy and reflects our philosophy of learning: Sit down at the computer and start at Chapter 1. You'll find that not only do we introduce HTML right away, we also take you through what can be a particularly frustrating aspect of learning computer technology: the actual mechanics of files, folders, and applications. We describe exactly how to set up your environment to facilitate learning the technology, and we take you step-by-step through each new HTML capability. In later chapters, we show you how to integrate HTML capabilities in a Web site and publish it on the Web. Then, we tease you with some JavaScript and describe some other kinds of technologies you can learn too. Finally, we offer several chapters on using social networking sites already available, creating a blog using online templates, and maintaining your cybersafety. Generally, if you're interested in HTML, you'll want to start at Chapter 1 and work through the chapters sequentially. However, if you want to skip ahead and work on customizing your social networking site or creating a blog based on a template before learning HTML, feel free to do so.

Every chapter ends with a summary and a set of Challenge Questions. We encourage you to answer these questions on your own; some will be quite easy, others a bit more challenging. They are a great way to test yourself and see what you've learned. Many the answers are on our Web site (http://www.html-for-kids.com) but because some questions are more variable than others and depend on your actions, not every answer is provided online.

Now, we don't intend this book to be the only one you'll need to become proficient with HTML—far from it! If this book turns you on to HTML, you'll need any number of other, more comprehensive books that can provide the detail you'll need.

System Requirements

We assume you're using a Microsoft Windows® operating system; that is, a computer running Microsoft Windows 2000, Microsoft Windows XP, or Microsoft Vista. If so, you're probably using Microsoft Internet Explorer as your Web browser (but that shouldn't matter too much). If you're using a Macintosh, we've also added instructions for you. In general, modern operating systems like Windows and Mac OS X work in similar ways, so you shouldn't have much trouble regardless of which system you use. The main difference is that the screen shots in this book won't look exactly the same as what you see on the Mac.

One important note for Mac users: In this book we often ask you to "right click" on an item. Newer Macs have a two-button mouse that allows you to right click just like you would on a PC. However, older Macs use a one-button mouse that has no right click button. To create a right click on these older computers, simply hold down the "Control" key on your keyboard when you click your mouse. This is the same as a right click.

A Note on Browsers and Editors

The first section of this book was created on a desktop computer running the Windows XP operating system. We used Notepad, a simple text editor, to create the HTML files and Internet Explorer 7.0 to display them as Web pages. As you read this section, it should be clear that you could use any text editor to create the HTML file and the result should display on any Web browser. If you use a computer running Vista or a Macintosh or even a Linux computer, you should have little or no problem using this book, as long as you can create HTML files using an editor and run them in your browser. On the Macintosh, TextEdit, which comes preinstalled on every Mac, is similar to Notepad. Alternatively, if you want a free, "super charged" text editor for the Mac, you can download and install TextWrangler from Bare Bones Software at http://www.barebones.com/products/textwrangler. Any of the popular Web browsers for the Macintosh, such as Safari, Firefox, or Opera, will work fine with this book. In fact, some of the screen shots in this book incorporate browsers other than Internet Explorer, so you can see how almost everything you do on the Web looks the same, regardless of the browser you're using.

Some browsers, including Internet Explorer 7.0, have built-in security systems that may get in the way of some of your exploring (in particular, when you get to the JavaScript section). For example, so-called pop-ups or scripts may be blocked. If so, you should be notified and have the option of "Allowing Blocked Content" and you should be all set.

OK, let's get started!

Getting Started:

Your First HTML Page

Welcome

EVERYONE probably knows about the World Wide Web, also called the *Internet,* the Web, and even, in the "old days" (1995 or so) the Information Superhighway (which sounds pretty lame, even to my dad). My friends and I just call it the Internet, as in "Did you get that off the Internet?" and we, like you, have grown up with it. The Internet is a humongous communications network of linked computers all around the world. Once you log on to the Internet, you can access a virtually unlimited amount of information from any of the computers on the network.

Everybody we know uses the Internet to browse (that is, go to different Web sites) for information for homework, hobbies, and games. I've used it to find out about magic tricks, get trading card information

This chapter will:

→ introduce you to basic concepts and terminology, such as HTML, tags, and Web browsers;

→ explain how to use Notepad (or TextEdit, if you're on a Mac) to create HTML files;

→ show you how to organize your work in one folder so that everything is easy to work with; and

→ help you create your first HTML Web page.

and cheat codes for video games, find helpful information for my home-work, view cool animations, watch the latest viral videos, check local movie times, play interactive games, and chat with other teens located all over the world. My Dad uses it to get news (boring—well, usually); check the stock market; buy stuff from online companies; find out about animals, nature, and hiking (my Dad's a real outdoors nut); and do his work as a computer scientist. Jennifer uses it to stay logged in to her university courses, chat with friends on social networking sites, read (and write) online journals or blogs, and find research sources for her writing projects.

You should be familiar with the terms *Web page* and *browsing,* because that's how you use the Internet. As you know, a Web site is a collection of Web pages hosted by a person, business, or organization. Each different screen you open on the Web site is a Web page. Browsing is how you get from one Web site to another, by typing in a URL (address) or clicking on a link. (We'll talk more about links in Chapter 5.)

Probably some of you have heard of HTML, and maybe you even know that that's how Web pages are created. Some of you have probably even created your own Web pages using Web site "wizards" and tools on your computer or online. These ways of creating Web pages are fairly easy—all you have to do is to enter the information you want on your page as prompted, make the selections you want, and voilà! You have a Web page. But there is a downside: Not only is it not quite as easy as it seems at first, but you don't learn what's actually going on. This is a problem, as far as we're concerned.

This part of the book is about how to create Web pages by writing HTML directly. HTML stands for "hypertext markup language," and hypertext means text with links in it, like the buttons on Web pages that send you from one page to another. HTML is a language that tells a Web browser what to draw and display on your computer screen. Writing HTML is really easy and really fun, and it allows you to make your Web page look exactly the way you want it to on any computer using a browser. That's one of the really cool features of HTML—it works on any kind of computer that can run a modern Web browser.

The other cool thing about writing HTML is that it's just the beginning of learning other nifty stuff like JavaScript, XML, and Java. I've done little bit of stuff like this, and it's really fun. I'll be showing you a little JavaScript near the end of this book.

One cool way to build a Web page that really reflects who you are as a teen is to create your own online journal, or Weblog (blog). Blogging is growing steadily as a way for teens (and adults) to discuss everything from their political views, to what they had for lunch, to their favorite books and movies, to which teachers are hardest (or easiest). Chapter 2 will definitely help you get started with an online journal, and Chapter 10, which discusses blogging specifically, will be useful to understanding what this new trend is all about.

But, because I'm a teen, and you guys are teens, I know that you might not be interested in just creating your own page. You might be reading this book to get more information about how you can interface with Web sites that already exist, such as social networking sites like MySpace and Facebook. If that's the case, check out Chapter 9. It will give you a lot of advice for taking the prebuilt platforms in MySpace and Facebook and really personalizing them to reflect who you are as an individual. It also will detail the many applications (or apps) that you can add to your pages to both interact with your friends, and express your personality, likes, and dislikes. This chapter also will show you how to use your new HTML knowledge to customize your social networking homepages.

Finally, because we are teens that live with the Internet daily, it's sometimes hard for us to understand why our parents worry about how much time we spend online. They have some good reasons to worry too—more and more teens are getting into trouble through contacts they've made over the Internet. Cybersafety will make your parents' happy, that's for sure, but it also might be the key to helping your protect yourself (and your identity). Chapter 11 talks all about how you can enjoy the Web, while staying safe. You don't want some random person stealing your identity, do you? Can there be two of you in this world? Read this chapter, and you'll be well-prepared to answer your parents' questions and ensure your protection.

Setting Up the Basics

The first thing you need to do is to create a folder for your work. We suggest you put it on the desktop, the main computer screen. You probably know how to do this, but in case you don't, it's easy. Just right-click (click the right mouse button and hold it down), and a little menu will appear. Scroll down to "New," then over to "Folder" (on the Mac, the menu item will be named "New Folder"). When you click on "Folder," a folder named "New Folder" will appear. You can rename the folder anything you want to call it by right-clicking on the folder and scrolling down to "Rename." Now, the name of the folder is highlighted, and you can change it by typing in a new name (and moving the cursor with the mouse or arrow keys if you like). *Note:* "Rename" is right under "Delete," which can cause a problem if you're not careful. Figure 1.1 shows what this looks like on our computer, with a new folder already created and renamed "My HTML." On the Mac, you can click on the new folder to select it, then click on the folder's name to highlight it, and then just type the new name.

FIGURE 1.1.
A Windows desktop, showing the menus you use to create a new folder.
You can see a new "My HTML" folder in the upper left. (You can put your folder anywhere on the desktop you like.)

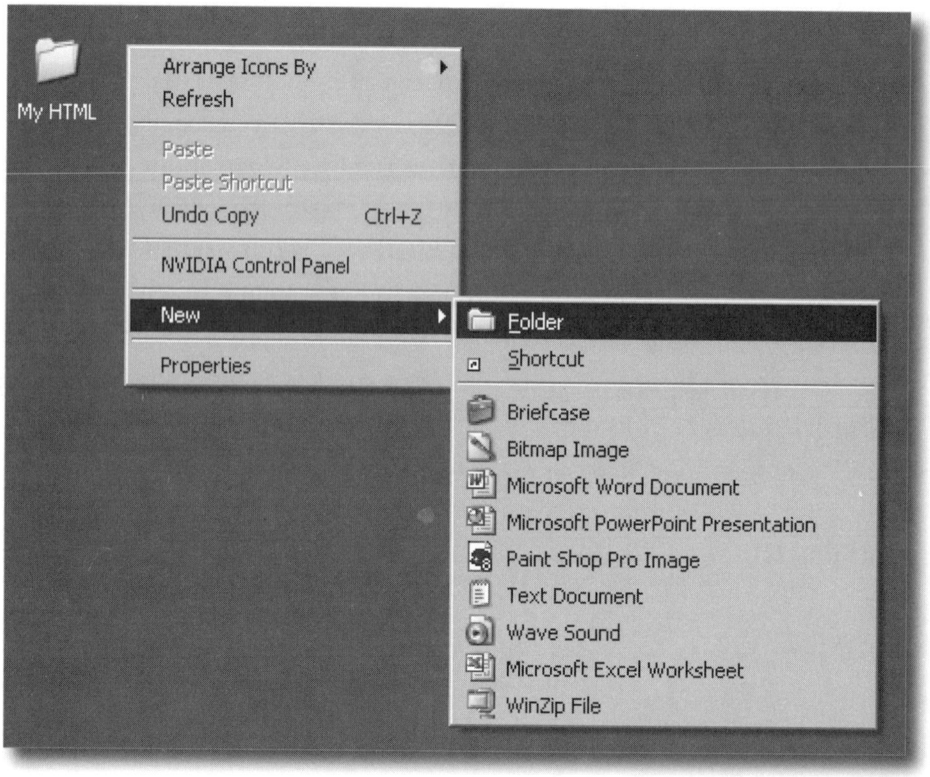

OK, now you've got your folder with a clever name like "My HTML." Now let's put into your folder some shortcuts to the two tools you will be using most often: Microsoft Notepad and your browser. A shortcut is just a link that you click on to open a file or program. On the Mac, a shortcut is called an *alias*, but it functions the same way. Your browser is what you use to get around the Internet. With a Windows computer, your browser is probably Internet Explorer, but you could use a different browser like Netscape Navigator, Firefox, or Opera. With a Macintosh computer, your browser most likely is either Safari or Firefox.

Assuming your new folder and the browser icon (picture) are both on the desktop, you can right-click on the browser icon, drag it to the folder, release, and choose "Create Shortcut(s) Here." Do the same thing with Notepad, which you should be able to find under Start → Programs → Accessories. (This means to click on the "Start" button in the lower left, scroll to "Programs," and scroll to "Accessories." You probably know this already.) Now your folder should look something like Figure 1.2 when you open it (double-click, or right-click and select "Open"). On the Mac, open your Applications folder, right click on TextEdit, and choose "Make Alias" from the pop-up menu. Do the same for Safari (or an other browser you want to use). Drag both of the new aliases from your Applications folder to your My HTML folder on your desktop.

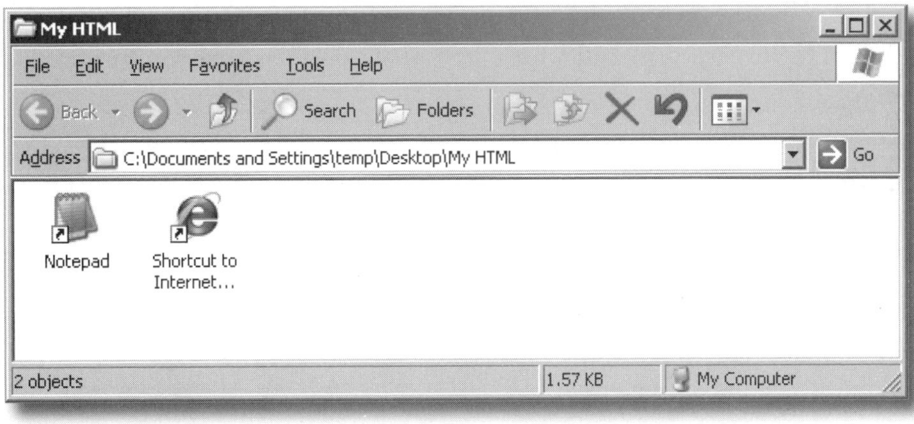

FIGURE 1.2. Open "My HTML" folder with shortcuts to Notepad and the Internet Explorer Web browser.

Creating a Basic HTML Page

OK, now you're ready to create your first HTML page. There are two parts to this process. First you need to create the HTML file that describes your page, and second you need to make it come up in your browser. Making the page appear in your browser is easy if you name the file properly.

Open up Notepad by double-clicking on the shortcut you just made. If you are using TextEdit on the Mac, double-click on the Alias for the Text-Edit application to open it, then when a blank document opens, click on the "Format" menu, and choose "Make Plain Text." Doing this will ensure that your new HTML file includes only text and no special formatting. If you plan to do a lot of HTML coding in TextEdit, you can set "Plain Text" as the default format in TextEdit's Preferences folder.

Then type in the following:

```
<html>
<head>
<title>Hello World</title>
</head>
<body>
Hello, World!
</body>
</html>
```

And, yes, we will tell you what all this means throughout this chapter.

The first thing to learn is that almost everything you just typed is a tag. A tag is a piece of text surrounded by angle brackets (< >). It is an HTML command that tells your browser what to do. To help you identify the tags used in this book, we've bolded them to make them stand out. The second thing to learn is that most tags come in pairs, with the second tag being the same as the first except for a slash like this: /. You can think of the / as meaning "stop." So, if one tag says < html >, a bit later you'll see an < /html > tag. One way to think about this is the first tag means "start the HTML section of the Web page" and the second means "stop the HTML section of the Web page." Tags are important for organization and to keep the meaning clear. (It's also important to get into the habit of using these tags, and this book will teach you that.)

> ### ⓘ Try This!
>
> By the way, the background of the desktop is really easy to change. Here's how: If you right-click your mouse on the background and scroll down to "Properties," you'll get a "Display Properties" menu. There's a bunch of stuff here, but there should be a tab for "Background." It will allow you to choose from a set of background images, preview each one, and choose whatever picture you want for your background. Try it!
>
> On the Mac, simply right-click on the desktop background and choose "Change Desktop Background . . ." from the menu that pops up. This brings up the Desktop & Screen Saver preference window, and this is where you can specify all kinds of desktop images and screen savers for your Mac. You can even use a picture you get off the Internet, or from a scanner or digital camera, for your desktop background. Can you see how?

Every HTML program has to be surrounded by the < html > and < /html > tags. This is what indicates to your browser that you are using HTML.

Next, there is a < head > section and within the head a title. ("Head" stands for heading, and why they don't just let you type "heading," we don't know.) The < title > tag just gives your Web page a title. (Really? Amazing, isn't it?) Whatever is between the < title > tags shows up on the little colored strip (sometimes called the title bar) that you see at the very top of your browser window. Because you typed "Hello World" between the < title > and < /title > tags, "Hello World" will show up at the top of your window.

> ### ⓘ Check It Out!
>
> Every one of the examples in this book is on our Web site at http://www.html-for-kids. com.

Finally, there's the body. Under the < body > tag is where you put all of the stuff that will appear on your Web page. This is a good time to bring to mind the real purpose of a Web page: It's to provide, present, or display information. Because the most basic kind of information on the Web is text, a basic Web page consists of some text. In the example, we've put just two words: "Hello, World!" If you like, you can type any words you choose here and you'll see them displayed on your Web page.

Displaying Your Page

OK, now that you understand what you typed into Notepad or Text-Edit, how do you get the browser to recognize the HTML and do what you've told it to do? It's pretty easy: All you have to do is to save the file with the proper kind of name. This takes a couple of steps. First, select "Save As" from the "File" menu of your open document, and the form shown in Figure 1.3 pops up (this is called a dialog box).

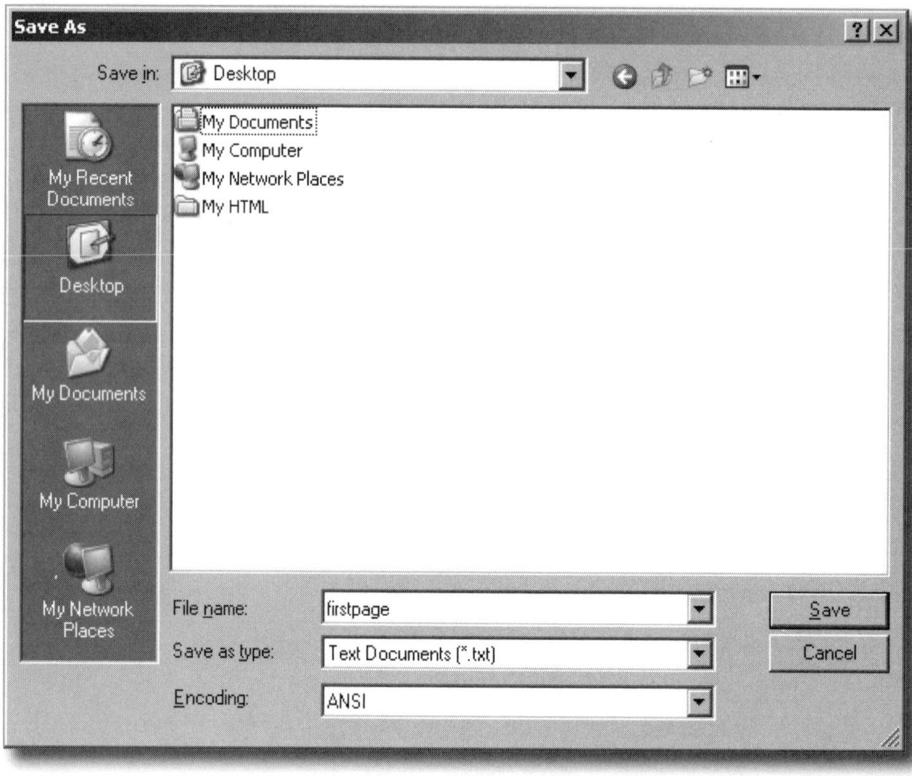

FIGURE 1.3. " Save As" dialog box in Notepad.

At the top of the dialog box you'll see "Save in:" and a small box. You have to make sure the folder you created in the first part of this chapter shows in this box. Select the little downward arrow tab on the right and you'll get a list of folders on your desktop. Figure 1.4 shows the folders on our desktop, with the My HTML folder we created for our Web pages. On the Mac, "Save As" works in a similar way. The "Save As" dialog box includes a way to specify where a file will be saved. Click on the "Where" pop-up menu and locate your My HTML folder (it should be located on your desktop).

Scroll down to My HTML, or whatever you called your folder. (See Figure 1.4; It should be indented under "Desktop" because it's on the desktop.) Click once and the file name should show up in the "Save in" box. You're all set with this part.

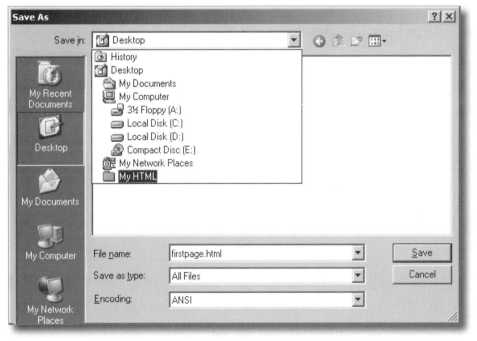

FIGURE 1.4.
Choosing the right folder to save your Web page in. Note that the "Save as type" box at the bottom of the window has been set to "All Files."

Now you need to save your file with a name ending with the file extension ".html." (A file extension is three or four letters after a period at the end of the file name.) To do this, you have to change the "Save as type" box to "All Files." (Again, click on the downward arrow and select the "All Files" choice.) Then, in the "File name" box, type "firstpage.html" and hit the "Save" button. Your file will be written into your HTML folder and will magically have the browser icon, which is the icon for HTML files (see Figure 1.5). On the Mac, just change the "File Format:" in the "Save As" dialog box to "HTML." The Mac will automatically add the correct extension to your file.

FIGURE 1.5. Open My HTML folder containing the saved "firstpage" file.

Now, if you double-click on the "firstpage" file, your Web browser will start right up and show you what's in the file, like you see in Figure 1.6.

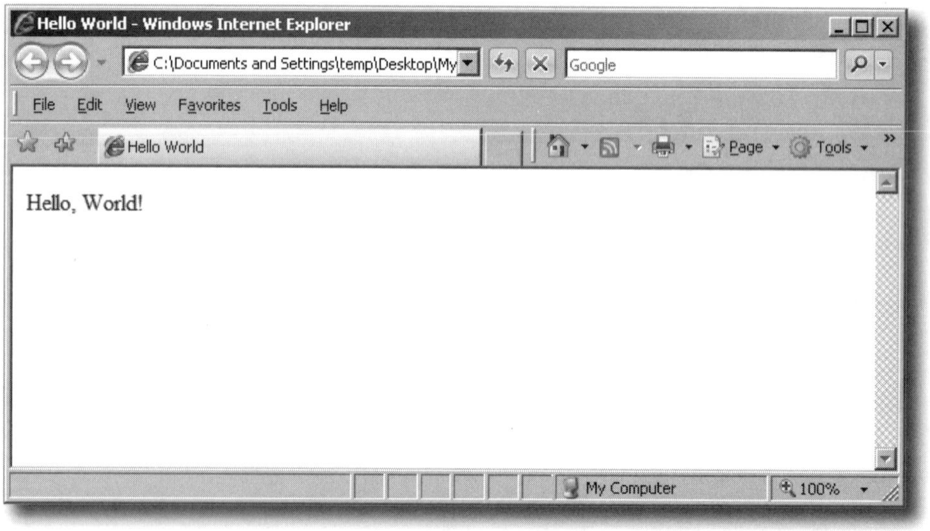

FIGURE 1.6. Open "firstpage" file showing the Web page you created.

Congratulations! You've created your first Web page. Before you start celebrating, though, try two more things. First, see the title at the top of the page where it says "Hello World—Microsoft Internet Explorer"? Let's change that to a different title. Second, let's put more text in the body of the Web page, so you can see how the text starts wrapping.

To make these changes, you will have to open your "firstpage" file in Notepad again. But wait a minute! Because you renamed your file "first-page.html," it now appears with a browser icon. If you just double-click on the file, it will open in your browser. So, how do you open it using Notepad instead? Put your cursor on the file and, once again, you can use the good old right-click method. But this time select "Open With," then "Choose Program." This will bring up the window you see in Figure 1.7.

Scroll down until you see Notepad (as shown) and click on it. Do not check the "Always use this program to open these files" checkbox at the bottom of the dialog box. Now, every time you need to edit the file, right-click on it. Notepad should be available under the "Open With" menu item. On the Mac, this process is almost exactly the same; however, TextEdit should automatically be on the list of available applications when you choose "Open With."

Start up Notepad or TextEdit again and change what follows the < **title** > tag to "This is my first Web page," so that this phrase will appear in the title bar. Second, still in Notepad, type something a bit longer than "Hello, World!" in the body section. For example, "Benjamin and Peter Selfridge have written an awesome book with the help of Jennifer Osburn, and I hope they sell a gazillion copies and make tons of money and the dad (Peter) should absolutely give the son (Ben) at least half of the money they earn so he can buy lots of video games and other books on cool technologies, and I guess putting some of it into his college fund is a good idea." You'll see that the text wraps from the first line onto the next lines. If you change the size of your browser window, you'll see that the text wrapping changes automatically. We're going to use this characteristic in the next chapter.

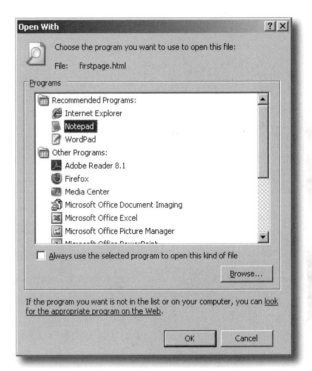

FIGURE 1.7.
"Open With" dialog box with Notepad selected.

Summary

In this chapter, we've covered how to set up your computer desktop with a folder to hold all of your work and shortcuts to the two main tools you'll use, Notepad and your browser. Then, we showed you how to create your first Web page by typing in a few lines of HTML primarily as tags, which are HTML commands. Finally, we showed you how to display the Web page in your browser by renaming it with the ".html" file extension. You're off and running!

☞ Challenge Questions

→ Take your first Web page file ("firstpage.html") and copy it and rename it. (How about "page2.html"?) Now open the copy using Notepad and type in a couple of sentences separated by a couple of blank lines. Then display the file using your browser. What happens?

→ Change the text between the <**title**> and </**title**> tags to anything you want. What happens when you display the page in your browser?

→ Now remove the </**title**> tag and display the page again. What happens? Why?

→ Right-click on your desktop and change the background.

ⓘ Did You Know?

Every piece of information in your computer is stored in a file. Even a folder is a file. Files typically have a name and an extension. The extension is the three or four letters after the . at the end of the file name. For example, in the file called "historypaper.doc," the *file name* is "historypaper" and the *extension* is "doc." The extension determines what application the computer will use to open a file. You probably know that Microsoft Word opens ".doc" files, Notepad opens ".txt" files, and your browser opens ".html" files.

Many people (even Mac users) don't realize that the Mac uses these same file extensions. That's because, out-of-the-box, the Mac hides them. To view these extensions, just click on the "Finder" icon on your dock. Navigate to the "Finder" menu in the upper left corner of your desktop. Select "Preferences" and then click on "Advanced." Here, you can click on the box in front of "Show all file extensions," and your Mac will do just that from here on out.

2

Fun With Fonts:

Creating an Online Journal

Creating a Personal Journal

WHY in the world would anyone want to create a journal on the Web? Well, by "personal journal" we don't necessarily mean a diary with all your biggest secrets in it. We just mean a bunch of information that you'd like to put in one place, like a report. So, we're going to pretend that you participate in baseball and you've been assigned to write a report on each game. Sound good? (Of course, who knows, maybe you really *are* a baseball nut.) If you really do want to create a journal that's more like a

This chapter will:

→ explain how to do your work with Notepad and your browser open side-by-side, which makes Web page creation easier;

→ show you how to add spaces and paragraphs to your work to improve its appearance;

→ introduce heading tags that help you organize your Web page;

→ show you how to change the color and style of your fonts and play with the spacing of your text to create an attractive Web page; and

→ show you how to put it all together to create an online journal.

diary, check out Chapter 10, on blogging, which is a trendy way of saying "online diary."

The first thing to do is to create a new file for your journal. The easiest (and thus almost always the best) way to do this is just to copy and rename an HTML file you've already created, such as your "firstpage.html" file. To do this, open up the folder that you created in the last chapter, position the mouse over the "firstpage" icon, hold down the right mouse button, and drag it over to an empty part of the folder. When you release the button, a menu will pop up that looks like the one in Figure 2.1.

FIGURE 2.1.
Making a copy of a file by dragging the icon.

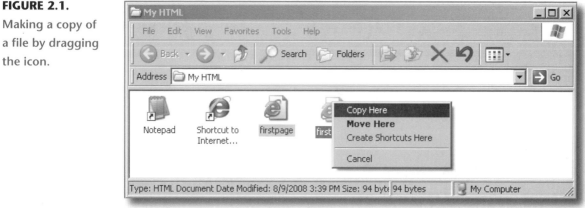

The menu gives you a choice to "Copy," "Move," or "Create a Shortcut." You want to select "Copy." You'll get a new file and icon (the little picture that stands for the file) that says "Copy of firstpage." On the Mac, just right click on your original file and select "Duplicate" from the pop-up menu. A duplicate of your "firstpage.html" file will be created that is named "firstpagecopy.html. Now you can rename the new file by right-clicking over it so that the pull-down menu appears as shown in Figure 2.2.

FIGURE 2.2.
Renaming the copied file.

Select "Rename" (down near the bottom); the menu will disappear and the cursor will be positioned inside the text under the file icon. Now you can type in a new name for your file. Rename your file "myjournal1." On the Mac, you can click on the file to select it, then click on the file's name to highlight it, and then just type the new name, "myjournal1." (By the way, since you did this in the first chapter and again here, from now on we'll assume that you know how to copy and rename files.)

After you've created the copy, open it using Notepad or TextEdit as we described on page X in Chapter 1 (remember, right-click and select "Open With" then "Notepad"). Now leave all of the HTML tags in place, just deleting the text between the tags. Type in an account of your baseball team, maybe something like the one in Figure 2.3, and then save the file.

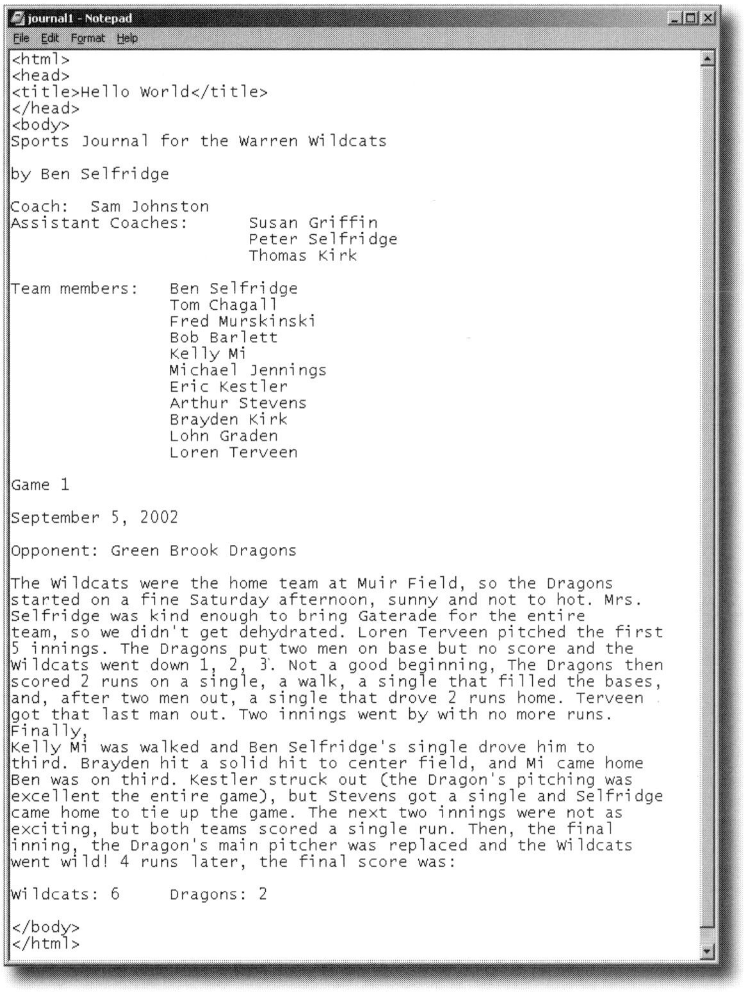

FIGURE 2.3.

Sample text for a journal created in Notepad.

But, now, here's a problem: When you double-click on the icon to bring up the file in your browser, the result is what you see in Figure 2.4.

FIGURE 2.4. How the journal in Figure 2.3 looks in your browser.

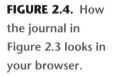

Sports Journal for the Warren Wildcats by Ben Selfridge Coach: Sam Johnston Assistant Coaches: Susan Griffin Peter Selfridge Thomas Kirk Team members: Ben Selfridge Tom Chagall Fred Murskinski Bob Barlett Kelly Mi Michael Jennings Eric Kestler Arthur Stevens Brayden Kirk Lohn Graden Loren Terveen Game 1 September 5, 2003 Opponent: Green Brook Dragons The Wildcats were the home team at Muir Field, so the Dragons started on a fine Saturday afternoon, sunny and not too hot. Mrs. Selfridge was kind enough to bring Gatorade for the entire team, so we didn't get dehydrated. Loren Terveen pitched the first 5 innings. The Dragons put two men on base but didn't score, and the Wildcats went down 1, 2, 3. Not a good beginning. The Dragons then scored 2 runs on a single, a walk, a single that filled the bases, and, after two men out, a single that drove 2 runs home. Terveen got that last man out. Two innings went by with no more runs. Finally, Kelly Mi was walked and Ben Selfridge's single drove him to third. Brayden Kirk hit a solid hit to center field, and Mi came home. Ben was on third. Kestler struck out (the Dragons' pitching was excellent the entire game), but Stevens got a single and Selfridge came home to tie up the game. The next two innings were not as exciting, but both teams scored a single run. Then, in the final inning, the Dragon's main pitcher was replaced and the Wildcats went wild! 4 runs later, the final score was: Wildcats: 7 Dragons: 3

Hmm. That wasn't quite what we had in mind. There must be some kind of solution.

Making Breaks and Paragraphs

Aha! The answer is breaks and paragraphs.

A break (making the text start on a new line) is done using the break tag < **br** >, and a paragraph, which is really a break then a blank line, is < **p** >. Neither of these tags has an ending tag; that is, you don't need to use < /**p** > or < /**br** >. (However, in future versions of HTML, the < /**p** > tag may be required. Don't forget that HTML is always evolving.)

We still need to figure out what both of these tags do exactly, and how to add them so that they will help our journal look better. (Our main goal in this book is to help you understand what's going on, instead of just having you copy down a bunch of stuff. Copying is easy. Understanding is much more powerful . . . and more fun!)

First, put < **br** >s in your "myjournal1" file wherever you want to start a new line. Here's the top part of the file as an example:

```
<html>
<head>
<title>Hello World</title>
</head>
<body>
Sports Journal for the Warren Wildcats
<br>
by Ben Selfridge
<br>
Coach: Sam Johnston
Assistant Coaches:      Susan Griffin
                        Peter Selfridge
                        Thomas Kirk
<br>
Team members:           Ben Selfridge
                        Tom Chagall
```

Figure 2.5 shows what you get in your browser if you do that in the appropriate places.

Although this clearly is an improvement, it's still not quite what we want. Before we fix it, let's make sure we understand what we did. The break tag (< **br** >) makes the text after it start on a new line. This is the first step toward properly formatting our journal (that is, making it look good).

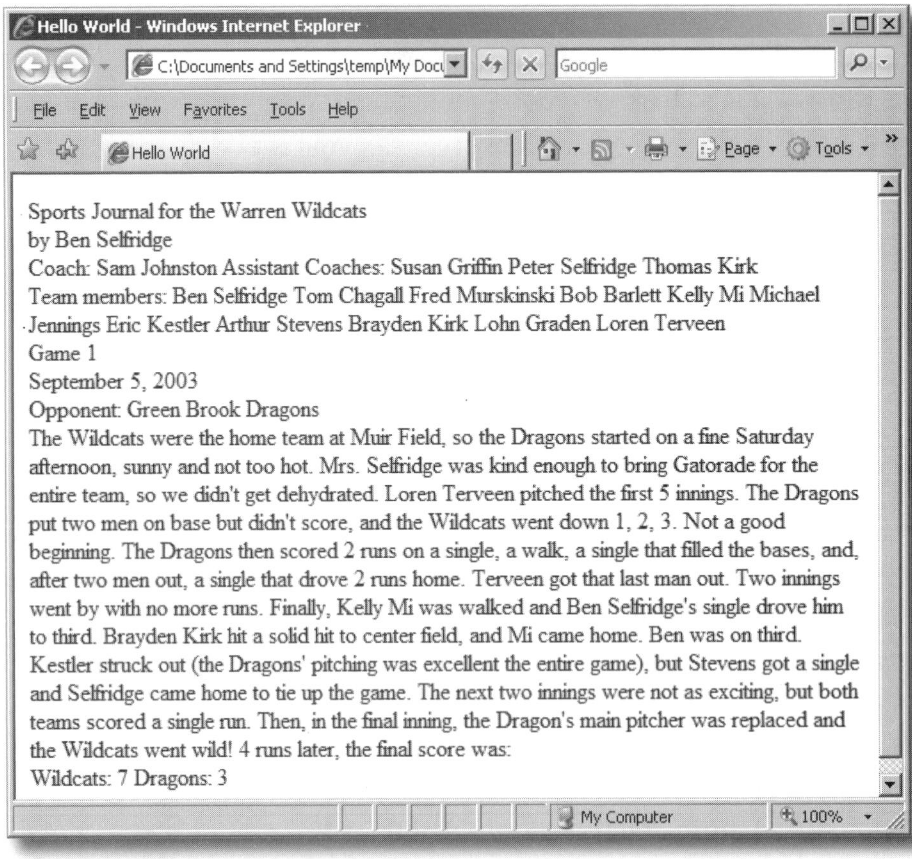
Hello World - Windows Internet Explorer
C:\Documents and Settings\temp\My Docu
Google
File Edit View Favorites Tools Help
Hello World
Page Tools
Sports Journal for the Warren Wildcats
by Ben Selfridge
Coach: Sam Johnston Assistant Coaches: Susan Griffin Peter Selfridge Thomas Kirk
Team members: Ben Selfridge Tom Chagall Fred Murskinski Bob Barlett Kelly Mi Michael Jennings Eric Kestler Arthur Stevens Brayden Kirk Lohn Graden Loren Terveen
Game 1
September 5, 2003
Opponent: Green Brook Dragons
The Wildcats were the home team at Muir Field, so the Dragons started on a fine Saturday afternoon, sunny and not too hot. Mrs. Selfridge was kind enough to bring Gatorade for the entire team, so we didn't get dehydrated. Loren Terveen pitched the first 5 innings. The Dragons put two men on base but didn't score, and the Wildcats went down 1, 2, 3. Not a good beginning. The Dragons then scored 2 runs on a single, a walk, a single that filled the bases, and, after two men out, a single that drove 2 runs home. Terveen got that last man out. Two innings went by with no more runs. Finally, Kelly Mi was walked and Ben Selfridge's single drove him to third. Brayden Kirk hit a solid hit to center field, and Mi came home. Ben was on third. Kestler struck out (the Dragons' pitching was excellent the entire game), but Stevens got a single and Selfridge came home to tie up the game. The next two innings were not as exciting, but both teams scored a single run. Then, in the final inning, the Dragon's main pitcher was replaced and the Wildcats went wild! 4 runs later, the final score was:
Wildcats: 7 Dragons: 3
My Computer
100%

FIGURE 2.5. How the journal text looks in your browser with breaks (<br>) inserted.

Now try replacing all the
s with <p>s, to see what happens; a really easy way to do this in Notepad is to select Edit → Replace, and you'll get this form to fill out (we've filled it out in Figure 2.6).

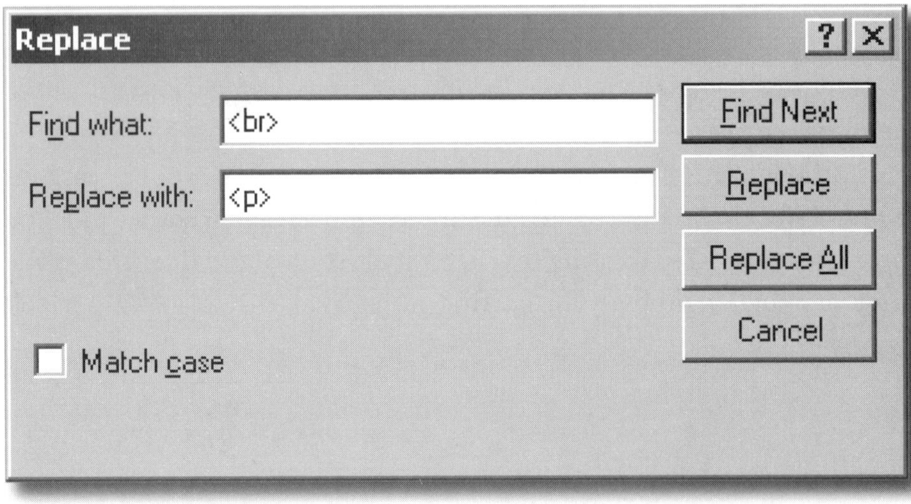
Replace
Find what:
Replace with: <p>
Find Next
Replace
Replace All
Cancel
Match case

FIGURE 2.6. Replacing the break tags (<br>) with paragraph tags (<p>).

Then click "Replace All" and you're all set. Notepad will go through your entire file and replace every occurrence of < br > with < p >, changing all of your break tags into paragraph tags. Now your Web page will look like what you see in Figure 2.7 when you open it in your browser.

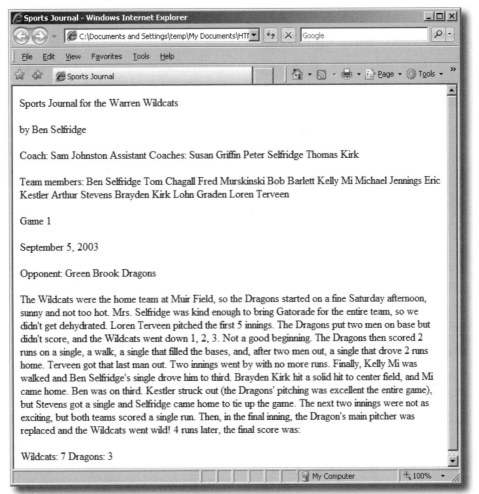

FIGURE 2.7. How the journal text looks in your browser with paragraphs (< p >) inserted.

This looks much better, but we want to make two things clear. First, just because we replaced all of the < br > tags with < p > tags doesn't mean that the < br > tag is useless. There are lots of times when you want a break without making a new paragraph—you'll see some examples later in the book. Second, before you do a global search and replace (that is, you replace all occurrences of one word or tag with another), you'd better be sure that this is really what you want to do. You can easily mess up your file in ways that are hard to fix. ("Undo" under the Edit menu in Notepad will undo a change if you realize you made a mistake right away.) But in this case, there are no examples of <br> that you want to keep, so you're OK.

I'll bet you can figure out how to use the <br> tag to make the coaches' and players' names appear in a list rather than run together, which will make the page look even better. (See? We told you <br> can be useful.) That leaves two other things to do: (1) Play with the size and style of the fonts (the style of the type), which we're about to do; and (2) indent lines, which we'll cover later.

ⓘ Did You Know?

You may have figured this out already, but HTML ignores so-called white space—including spaces, tabs, and even hard returns (the Enter key). This can be a bit confusing at first. It means, for example, that it doesn't make any difference whether tags are on their own line or not:

<h1>This is a heading</h1>
or <h1>
This is a heading </h1>
Either way, the text looks exactly the same.

Working With Notepad or TextEdit and Your Browser at the Same Time

Before we go on, we're going to show you a really cool way to learn HTML faster: Keep the Notepad or TextEdit file and the browser open at the same time. That is, open the Notepad file by right-clicking on the "myjournal1" icon and choosing Open With → Notepad (or TextEdit). You should get the file you typed in. Then, double-click the icon (which is the same as opening it using your browser), and you'll get the Web page. Now, you can change the html file, save the results using File → Save or Ctrl+S (Save or Command+S on the Mac), then hit the "Refresh" button on the browser.

Voilà! The browser shows the new Web page. This allows you to go back and forth, making changes in your Notepad file, saving them, then checking the result right away in the browser. This is a much more efficient way to work than opening only one application at a time.

Figure 2.8 is a shot of a screen that shows this.

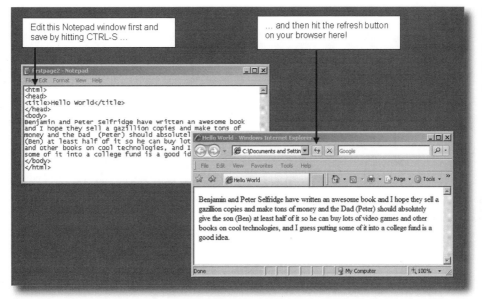

FIGURE 2.8. Working with Notepad and your browser open simultaneously.

Changing Font Size Using the Heading Tag

Do you know what a font is? If you've used word processing software, you probably do: A font is basically a certain kind of lettering, or technically a typeface, and there are hundreds if not thousands of them. Leaving the type of font alone, let's change the font size in the easiest way possible—with heading tags.

Heading tags are easy. There are six of them, with matching end tags, and they look like this:

```
<h1> </h1>       <h4> </h4>
<h2> </h2>       <h5> </h5>
<h3> </h3>       <h6> </h6>
```

You get the idea. A pair of heading tags makes the text between them bigger. So, < h1 > is the biggest size of heading, < h2 > the next biggest, and so on. To try out these tags, edit your "myjournal1" file and put heading tags around the text that you want to make larger. We'd suggest using heading 1 (< h1 >) for the title, heading 2 for the author, heading 3 for the "coach" and "team members" lines, and heading 2 for the line that says "Game 1." Here's how your tags will look in Notepad:

```
<html>
<head>
<title>My journal</title>
</head>
<body>
<h1>Sports Journal for the Warren Wildcats</h1>
<p>
<h2>by Ben Selfridge</h2>
<p>
<h3>Coach: Sam Johnston</h3>
<p>
<h3>Assistant Coaches:</h3>
<br>
Susan Griffin
<br>
Peter Selfridge
<br>
Thomas Kirk
<p>
```

Note that we've put in the < br > tags to separate the names, as we talked about earlier. Now, your Web page looks much, much better (see Figure 2.9).

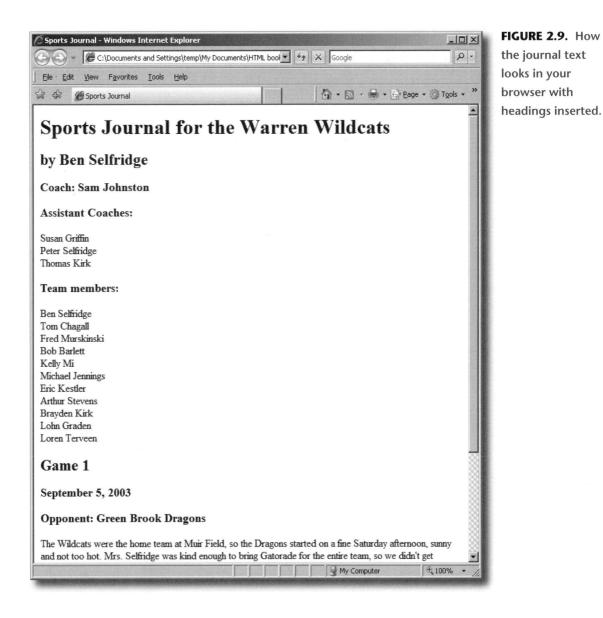

FIGURE 2.9. How the journal text looks in your browser with headings inserted.

Spicing Up Text: The Direct Method

At this point, our journal is looking pretty good. But, the actual text describing the game is starting to look a little tame, now that we've added headings of different sizes. Let's look at three other ways of changing the appearance of the text. (If you've used Microsoft Word, you're probably familiar with all three.) These are making text bold, italic, or underlined. And, yes, you can combine these. Let's take a look. Each type style has its own pair of tags, a beginning tag that goes in front of the text you want to change the appearance of, and an end tag that turns off the effect. These tags are particularly easy to remember:

```
Bold:            <b>  </b>
Italic:          <i>  </i>
Underline:       <u>  </u>
```

Let's make a really simple example. (From now on, we'll usually skip putting in the basic < html >, < body >, and other "boilerplate," or standard, tags in our examples. We assume you know how to put them in by now.) So here's some HTML:

```
<h3><u>Text Spice:</u></h3>
Here is some text that is <b>bold</b>, <i>italic</i>,
and <u>underlined</u>. And here's some text that is
formatted using <b><i><u>all three tags!</b>
</i></u>. Cool, huh?
```

Notice that we underlined the heading, to show you that you really can combine these tags with any other text tags. Just remember to think about a tag as meaning start, like this: < i > means "start italics," and you'll have an easier time remembering to include < /i > for "end italics." Figure 2.10 shows the many ways you can spice up text.

FIGURE 2.10.
Examples of bold, italic, and underlined text, and all three together.

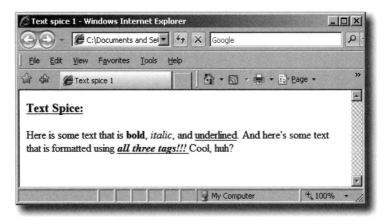

Spicing Up Text:
The Indirect Method

There's another way of spicing up text that we'll call the indirect method. We'll show you two ways of doing this: the emphasis tag and the strong tag. Both of these need the usual end tags. Here's how each one looks in Notepad:

```
I want to <em>emphasize</em> the word "emphasize."
I want the word "strong" to look <strong>strong
</strong>.
```

Now, if you go to the description of the game and surround every player's name with the emphasis tag, here's what the game description will look like (see Figure 2.11).

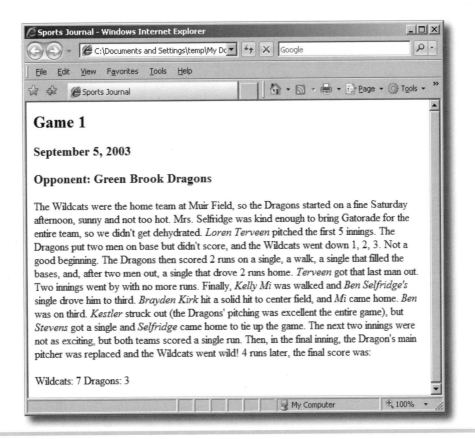

FIGURE 2.11. How the journal text looks in your browser with emphasis tags around players' names.

If you replace the emphasis tag with the strong tag (remembering to change the end tags too), you get Figure 2.12, which we think looks even better. (Can you remember how to do a global replace? See page 20.)

See page 20.

FIGURE 2.12.
How the journal text looks in your browser with strong tags around players' names.

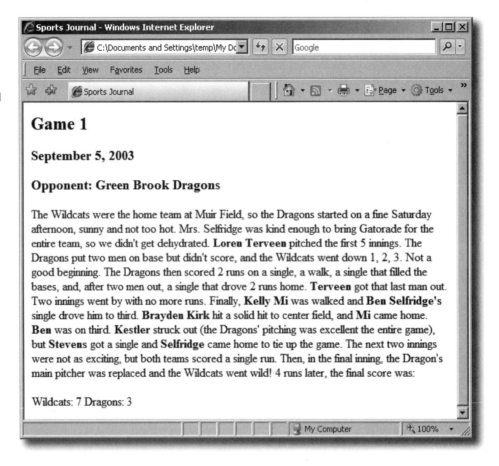

Sports Journal – Windows Internet Explorer

C:\Documents and Settings\temp\My Dc   Google

File   Edit   View   Favorites   Tools   Help

Sports Journal   Page ▾   Tools ▾

Game 1

September 5, 2003

Opponent: Green Brook Dragons

The Wildcats were the home team at Muir Field, so the Dragons started on a fine Saturday afternoon, sunny and not too hot. Mrs. Selfridge was kind enough to bring Gatorade for the entire team, so we didn't get dehydrated. **Loren Terveen** pitched the first 5 innings. The Dragons put two men on base but didn't score, and the Wildcats went down 1, 2, 3. Not a good beginning. The Dragons then scored 2 runs on a single, a walk, a single that filled the bases, and, after two men out, a single that drove 2 runs home. **Terveen** got that last man out. Two innings went by with no more runs. Finally, **Kelly Mi** was walked and **Ben Selfridge's** single drove him to third. **Brayden Kirk** hit a solid hit to center field, and **Mi** came home. **Ben** was on third. **Kestler** struck out (the Dragons' pitching was excellent the entire game), but **Stevens** got a single and **Selfridge** came home to tie up the game. The next two innings were not as exciting, but both teams scored a single run. Then, in the final inning, the Dragon's main pitcher was replaced and the Wildcats went wild! 4 runs later, the final score was:

Wildcats: 7 Dragons: 3

My Computer   100%

ⓘ Did You Know?

Be careful not to go nuts with different fonts and text effects. While they're fun to play with, too many different fonts make Web pages hard to read—a classic "newbie" mistake. Try sticking with a couple of fonts and a couple of colors. The goal is to create a slick-looking design, not a lot of clutter.

Fonts and the Font Tag

As the last example shows, there often are different ways of accomplishing the same thing in HTML, and we're going to see another example here. You've already learned how to make text larger using heading tags, but those tags don't let you enlarge just a few words inside a paragraph. You can do that using the font tag: < **font** >. As you'll see, you can add a number of attributes to this tag, including one to change the typeface and the color of the text. Attributes are just additional characteristics that go inside the tag. Here's a simple example:

```
<html>
<head>
<title>Font1</title>
</head>
<body>
Once upon a time there lived a small <font
face="Impact" size=5 color=purple> squirrel</font>
named Ziggy.
</body>
</html>
```

The font tag allows you to set the color of the type, the size, and the typeface. Here, we specify the typeface called Impact. The attributes are pretty straightforward, but it does help to know that there are seven sizes of fonts (**size=1**, **size=2**, and so on). Colors can be represented either by name (there are a bunch of names, including the standard colors such as red, green, blue, and so on) or by hexadecimal code (**#rrggbb**), although for our purposes, we'll just use color names. You can use these to create any color combination of red, green, and blue that you want.

Figure 2.13 shows what the preceding HTML looks like in your browser (minus the color, which doesn't show up in this book). When you do this exercise yourself, you'll see the color on your screen.

FIGURE 2.13.
Changing the
appearance of
a word using
the font tag and
attributes.

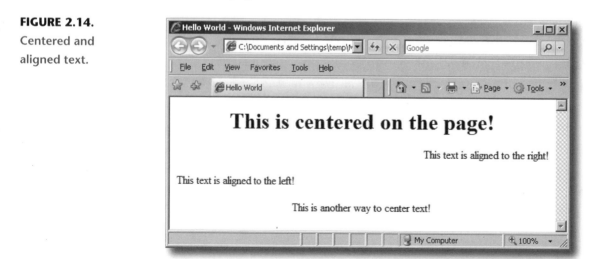

Once upon a time there lived a small **squirrel** named Ziggy.

ⓘ Try This!

To find out what fonts are available (at least on Internet Explorer), use the
Tools menu and select "Internet Options." At the bottom of the "General"
tab you'll see a button labeled "Fonts." Be sure to use these names in quotes
inside a <font> tag, as we've shown you.

Positioning Text on the Page

You can use lots of other tags to make your text look the way you
want it to. We're not going to go over all of them, but here are some tags
for positioning text on your page. Figure 2.14 shows what each one looks
like on a Web page.

FIGURE 2.14.
Centered and
aligned text.

This is centered on the page!

This text is aligned to the right!

This text is aligned to the left!

This is another way to center text!

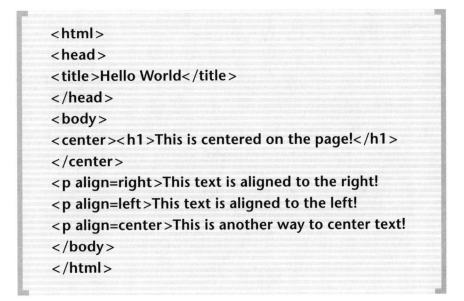

```
<html>
<head>
<title>Hello World</title>
</head>
<body>
<center><h1>This is centered on the page!</h1>
</center>
<p align=right>This text is aligned to the right!
<p align=left>This text is aligned to the left!
<p align=center>This is another way to center text!
</body>
</html>
```

Summary

Wow, you have made really great progress. You've learned how to create and nicely format an online journal using breaks and paragraphs, headings, and bold, italic, and underlined text. You also got a brief introduction to the < **font** > tag, which allows you change the typeface of a word, and you know how to center text or align it with the left or right edge of the screen. You also saw a really convenient way to work with Notepad and your browser open side-by-side.

☞ Challenge Questions

➔ What is the difference between the break tag < **br** > and the paragraph tag < **p** >?

➔ Take the journal file as we had it in Figure 2.5 and add breaks to separate the names of the coaches and assistant coaches.

➔ Create a page that uses all six heading tags so that the text "This is heading 1" appears in heading 1, the text "This is heading 2" appears in heading 2, and so on.

➔ Leave out an < **/h** > tag. What happens?

➔ Add bold to heading 3. What happens? Why?

Interesting Images:
Creating a Web Photo Album

3

Images and Image Files

WE think you'll agree that in the last chapter, things began to get interesting. Breaking the text into sections, adding heading tags, and using italics and bold for emphasis resulted in a really nice-looking Web page. However, the Web is about much more than just text, and putting images on your Web page is the first step toward multimedia Web content. (*Multimedia* means images, sounds, and even movie clips.)

First it's worthwhile to understand what a digital image really is. It's really just a big array of numbers, where each number represents the amount of color in a pixel, or picture element. Let's look at an example. To keep things simple at first, imagine a black-and-white image of black stripes on a white background with dimensions of 100 by 100 pixels

This chapter will:

→ explain what an image file is and how to get and save images off the Web;

→ show you how to put images onto your Web page and put text next to and around them;

→ provide guidelines for using images; and

→ show you how to put everything you know together to create a photo album on the Web.

(100 pixels wide by 100 pixels high). The stripes in our image will be 5 pixels wide and separated by 5 pixels. Figure 3.1 shows the image and then, blown up, the array of numbers that corresponds to part of it. Note that 0 means "no color," that is, black, and 255 means "all color," that is, white.

FIGURE 3.1. A simple image of black-and-white stripes, showing the pixels that make up the pattern.

```
255 255 255 255 255 0 0 0 0 0 255 255 255 255 255
255 255 255 255 255 0 0 0 0 0 255 255 255 255 255
255 255 255 255 255 0 0 0 0 0 255 255 255 255 255
255 255 255 255 255 0 0 0 0 0 255 255 255 255 255
255 255 255 255 255 0 0 0 0 0 255 255 255 255 255
255 255 255 255 255 0 0 0 0 0 255 255 255 255 255
255 255 255 255 255 0 0 0 0 0 255 255 255 255 255
255 255 255 255 255 0 0 0 0 0 255 255 255 255 255
255 255 255 255 255 0 0 0 0 0 255 255 255 255 255
255 255 255 255 255 0 0 0 0 0 255 255 255 255 255
255 255 255 255 255 0 0 0 0 0 255 255 255 255 255
255 255 255 255 255 0 0 0 0 0 255 255 255 255 255
255 255 255 255 255 0 0 0 0 0 255 255 255 255 255
```

What about color images? Well, every pixel is represented by three numbers, one for the red value, one for the blue value, and one for the green value. So, a pixel with the color purple would be represented by the numbers 255, 255, 0, that is, all red, all blue, and no green.

Images are stored on your computer as files, just like any other kind of data. There are many different kinds of image formats, or ways of storing images, which are indicated by the file extension, as discussed in Chapter 1. The most common formats are bitmap, stored with the extension .bmp; GIF, stored with the extension .gif; portable network graphics, stored with the extension .png; and JPEG, stored with the extension .jpg. Typically, Web images are either .gif or .jpg (GIF or JPEG format).

Where can you get images? Two possible sources are a scanner or a digital camera. We're not going to talk about these, because the end result is the same: you have an image file that you can put on your Web page. Another way to create an image is to use a drawing program like Microsoft Paint, which comes with every Windows PC (at least as far as we know). You can usually find it under Start → Programs → Accessories → Paint. If you create an image using Paint, you should save it using GIF or JPEG formats, not bitmap. The file will be much smaller that way, which is especially important if you plan on using the image in a Web page.

The easiest way to get an image is to take it from the Web itself. But, be careful how you use images from the Web because many of them are copyrighted. This means that someone owns the image, and you can't use it without that person's permission. Look for images that are in "public domain"; that means anyone is free to use them. To save an image from the Web, all you have to do is to right-click on it, then select "Save Picture As" ("Save Image As . . ." on the Mac). Be sure to save the image as whatever type shows up in the dialogue box. We suggest you save all of your images in a separate folder within your HTML folder. Call this new folder "images."

(i) Did You Know?

Your computer almost certainly has lots of image files stored on it already. You can search for these using the extensions we talked about: .gif, .jpg, and .bmp. Go to Start → Find → Files or folders. On a Mac, you can do similar searches using Spotlight (click on the magnifying glass on the top right of your screen or type Command+F in the Finder). If you are running Leopard (the newest version of the Mac's operating system) you can use the "All Images" smart folder on the lower left side of a Finder window's sidebar (look for the smart folders under "SEARCH FOR"). That smart folder (along with others) comes preinstalled on Leopard.

Using the Basic Image Tag to Put an Image on a Web Page

Now that you know a little about images and image files, let's take the first step toward putting an image on a Web page. Let's first use familiar tags to create a new page with a title and a heading. As always, we'll put in some extras (underlining and italics) that you've already learned.

```
<html>
<head>
<title>My dad in the morning</title>
</head>

<body>
<h1 align = center><b><i>Hey!!! Look at my dad when
he first wakes up in the morning!!!</b></i></h1>
</body>
</html>
```

Call this file image1.html. This results in a page like the one you see in Figure 3.2.

FIGURE 3.2.
Heading for
image1 file.

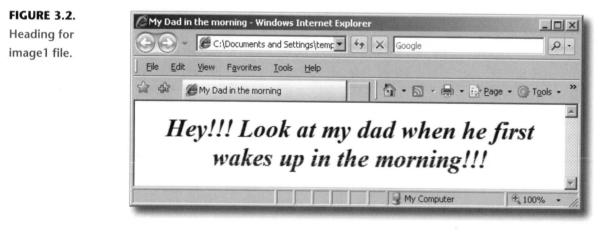

Now let's add an image tag in the simplest possible form. We're going to add an image file called "sillydad.gif," which is found on our computer in the images folder within the My HTML folder.

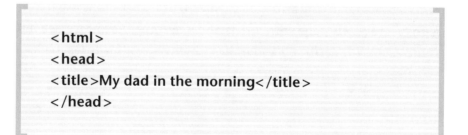

```
<html>
<head>
<title>My dad in the morning</title>
</head>
```

```
<body>
<h1 align=center><b><i>Hey!!! Look at my dad when
he first wakes up in the morning!!!</b></i></h1>
<img src="images/sillydad.gif">
</body>
</html>
```

Note that "images/sillydad.gif" tells the computer to go to the images subfolder and open the file "sillydad.gif." Figure 3.3 shows the result.

Now try the same thing using an image file you have saved in your images folder.

FIGURE 3.3.

A Web page containing an image.

Positioning Images and Combining Them With Text

Now that you've managed to put an image on a Web page (it wasn't too hard, was it?), let's do something a bit more complicated. Let's say we have three images that we want to put on a Web page with some text by each picture. (By the way, to make my three pictures, I scanned one picture of my dad, which I called "dad1.gif." Then I copied this file twice, and renamed the copies "dad2.gif" and "dad3.gif." Finally, I used Microsoft Paint to draw on the copies. If you use a Mac and want to edit images, you can download and install the free application, Seashore, from http://seashore.sourceforge.net). Seashore packs a lot of image editing power into a free application.

For our first try, use this HTML:

```
<html>
<head>
<title>3Dads</title>
</head>
<body>
These are three pictures of my handsome dad!
<img src="images/dad1.gif">
<img src="images/dad2.gif">
<img src="images/dad3.gif">
</body>
</html>
```

Figure 3.4 shows what we get.

FIGURE 3.4. A Web page with three images that aren't where we want them.

Several things are not quite the way we wanted them to look. First, the images are next to each other. (If we made the Web page bigger, all three would be on the same line.) Second, the text, "These are three pictures of my handsome dad!" is positioned in an odd place and doesn't look very good.

> ### ⓘ Check It Out!
>
> **I'm sure you have used Google to search for Web pages, but did you know that you can use Google to search for images? Check out the Images tab on the main Google search page. As I mentioned above, be careful when using images you find with Google. They need to be in the public domain or made available for free use by the creator of the image.**

There's a reason why this happened that's kind of interesting and kind of stupid. HTML "thinks" an image is just like a single character, such as an "a" or "b." So, it puts the first image right after the "... handsome dad!" text, then the next image right after that, and the third image right after that. Just like with text, when the images don't all fit on the same line, the browser wraps them down to the next line.

If you were paying attention in Chapter 2, you might think of using the break (<br>) tag. Yes, you would be right; that would put each image on its own line. But, we're going to introduce another tag here, called the "rule" tag. It looks like this: < hr >, and stands for "horizontal rule." (Rule means line.) It has no end tag. The rule tag is sort of like a break or paragraph tag, except that it puts a line across the page, making a nice, handsome break. You can use it anywhere you want to make a new section.

So, let's add an < hr > tag before each < img > tag, and furthermore, let's make the first text a nice, big header. Here's the HTML to do this, and Figure 3.5 shows the result in your browser:

```
<html>
<head>
<title>3Dads</title>
</head>
```

```
<body>
<h1>These are three pictures of my handsome dad!
</h1>
<hr>
<img src="images/dad1.gif">
<hr>
<img src="images/dad2.gif">
<hr>
<img src="images/dad3.gif">
</body>
</html>
```

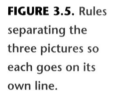

FIGURE 3.5. Rules separating the three pictures so each goes on its own line.

This looks much better, but we're still not done. Let's add some text next to each image:

```
<html>
<head>
<title>3Dads</title>
</head>
<body>
<h1>These are three pictures of my handsome dad!
</h1>
<hr>
<img src="images/dad1.gif">
Here he's about age 45.
<hr>
<img src="images/dad2.gif">
Here he's age 48—note the disappearing hair and
scraggly beard. He blames these changes on my
becoming a teenager.
<hr>
<img src="images/dad3.gif">
Here the burden of raising me has proved too much
and he's become weirded out and needs a nap. Ha! Ha!
</body>
</html>
```

ⓘ Try This!

Because you can change the color of the text in your Web page, you should be able to change the background color as well, right? And, yes, you can. Here's how:

```
<body bgcolor=blue>
```

Now, when we look at the page in our browser, we get Figure 3.6.

FIGURE 3.6. Text added next to each picture, with the middle text wrapping under the image.

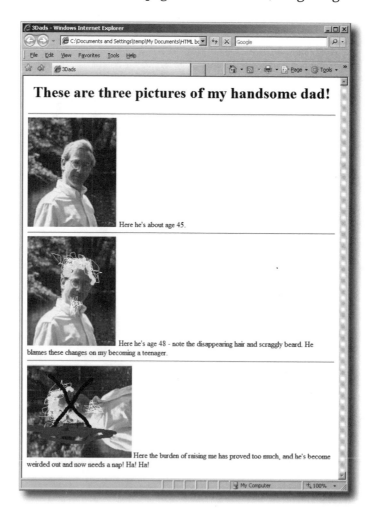

Once again, we notice a problem: the text for the middle picture wraps under the picture. Again, that's because HTML thinks of the image as a great big character, so the text just wraps around it when there's no more room on a line. Later, we'll learn about tables, which are the only good way to fix this. In the meantime, we'd be best off putting a paragraph (you remember, "< p >") before each line of text, and making all of the picture captions level 2 headings (< h2 >). Then we can use the center tag to center all of the images and all of the text at the same time.

```
<html>
<head>
<title>3Dads</title>
</head>
<body>
<h1>These are three pictures of my handsome Dad!
</h1>
<hr>
<center>
<img src="images/dad1.gif">
<p>
<h2>Here he's about age 45.</h2>
<hr>
<img src="images/dad2.gif">
<p>
<h2>Here he's age 48—note the disappearing hair
and scraggly beard. He blames these changes on my
becoming a teenager.
</h2>
<hr>
<img src="images/dad3.gif">
<p>
<h2> Here the burden of raising me has proved too
much, and he's become weirded out and now needs a
nap. Ha! Ha!</h2>
</center>
</body>
</html>
```

And now, we're done, as you see in Figure 3.7. (But note that this Web page is now so long that we can't display it all on one screen. Later in this book, we'll show you how to add links that take you down to other parts of the page.)

FIGURE 3.7.

Centering the entire page and making the text headings to improve the appearance.

Making an Image the Background of Your Web Page

This is so easy it's almost ridiculous. Remember the body tag that looks like this: < **body** >? Try this:

```
<body background="images/dad1.gif">
<font color=white>
<h1>THIS IS UNSPEAKABLY HIDEOUS!</h1>
```

Here's what happens: The image is repeated in both directions (up and down and side to side) as needed to fill the background of your Web page. Figure 3.8 shows what it looks like using my dad's picture. (This would be good for my dad's fan club, if he had one!)

FIGURE 3.8. Using an image as a Web page background.

Making Text Flow Around an Image

What we did before, giving each picture of my dad its own caption, is the kind of thing you'd do for a photo album. But what if you wanted to make the image part of the Web page and have the text wrap around it? It turns out that you can use the "align" tag to do this. Here's a quick example, where the beginning letter I is an image (Figure 3.9 also shows wrap-around text):

(i) Check It Out!

To find out what colors are available in HTML, use Google to search for a phrase like "HTML colors."

```
<html>
<head>
<title>Font1</title>
</head>
<body>
    <img src="images/i.gif" align=left>
    n the wild woods of Watchung, New Jersey,
    there lived a small <font face="Impact" size=5
    color=purple> squirrel</font> named Ziggy. He
    was a happy squirrel, partly because he lived in the
    woods near the Selfridges. They were very nice to
    him and always fed him chocolate-covered acorns
    (his favorite) and everything was wonderful until
    Ben Selfridge decided that it would be fun if Ziggy
    could be trained to be his servant. Dressed in a black
    tuxedo, Ziggy was now put to work bringing Ben
    birch beer and cupcakes, potato chips and spring
    water, and other . . .
</body>
</html>
```

FIGURE 3.9.

Making text wrap around an image.

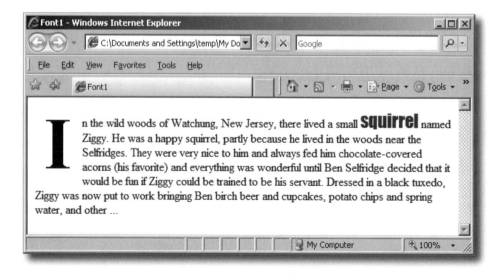

Summary

In this chapter we went far beyond working with mere text and explored how to put images on your Web page. First, we described a little bit about how images are actually stored on a computer, and then we built a simple Web page with an image using the < **img** > tag. Next we explored the process of putting three images on a single page and discovered that we need breaks in the form of rules between them. Then we demonstrated two other cool things: using an image as the background for a Web page and getting text to wrap around an image.

☞ Challenge Questions

→ We used Microsoft Paint (on the Mac, you can use Seashore) to create the little image of the capital *I* in Figure 3.9. Try doing this with another letter, and try to make the background of the image match the background in your Web page.

→ We also used Paint to rotate the third dad image in Figure 3.7. Can you see how?

→ Experiment with different colors for your Web page background and text. Which ones work well together?

4

Likeable Lists and Terrific Tables:
Making Your Page Look Really Cool

Creating and Using Lists

LET'S take an example from Chapter 2, where we created the beginnings of an online journal. Here's just the part that lists the assistant coaches (Figure 4.1 shows the resulting Web page):

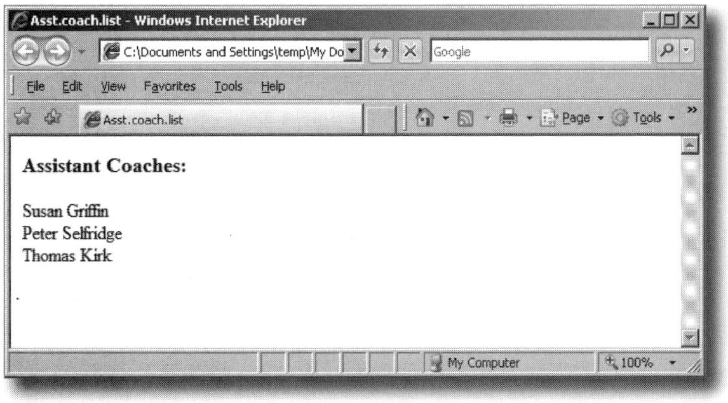

Assistant Coaches:

Susan Griffin
Peter Selfridge
Thomas Kirk

FIGURE 4.1. List of assistant coaches set up with breaks.

This chapter will:

→ show you how to make text look nice by putting it into several varieties of lists;

→ introduce tabular data and show you what this is good for; and

→ redo the images of my dad so the text is beside each image.

```
<html>
<head>
<title>Asst.coach.list</title>
</head>
<body>
<h3>Assistant Coaches:</h3>
Susan Griffin
<br>
Peter Selfridge
<br>
Thomas Kirk
<p>
</body>
</html>
```

Although this Web page is perfectly readable, you can make it look better using lists. The simplest kind of list in HTML is the unordered list (< **ul** >). All you have to do is to start the list with a < **ul** > tag, then start each line of the list with a < **li** > ("list item") tag. This method is nice because it requires fewer tags and looks much better than the method we used in Figure 4.1. Here's the HTML, and Figure 4.2 shows the resulting Web page.

FIGURE 4.2. List of assistant coaches set up as an unordered list.

```
<html>
<head>
   <title>Asst.coach.list</title>
</head>
<body>
<h3>Assistant Coaches:</h3>
   <ul>
      <li>Susan Griffin
      <li>Peter Selfridge
      <li>Thomas Kirk
   </ul>
</body>
</html>
```

Isn't that cool? Note how we indented the HTML code. We think this looks really nice and the added structure makes the code more readable.

Here's another way to make a list: an ordered list (< **ol** >), which numbers the list entries. Figure 4.3 shows how it looks.

FIGURE 4.3. An ordered list.

```
<html>
<head>
    <title>Ben's foods</title>
</head>
<body>
<h3>My favorite foods, from most to least favorite:
</h3>
    <ol>
        <li>Pizza
        <li>Pancakes
        <li>Dad's delicious snack plates
        <li>Popcorn
        <li>Chocolate-chip cookies
        <li>Carrots
        <li>Dad's overcooked steak
        <li>Virtually any leftovers
        <li>Dirt
    </ol>
</body>
</html>
```

You can do many other things with lists. For example, if you don't like using regular numbers (1, 2, 3, and so on) for the numbers, you can change them to letters or even Roman numerals! To do this, you add "**type=**" to the < **ol** > tag. For example:

< **ol type=A** > will use A, B, C . . .
< **ol type=a** > will use a, b, c . . .
< **ol type=I** > will use Roman numerals: I, II, III, . . .
< **ol type=i** > will use lowercase Roman numerals: i, ii, iii . . .

Why would anyone want to use Roman numerals in a list? Well, it might make sense if you make lists inside of lists (called *nesting*). Then, you can make an outline in the style you were probably taught in school.

(Note that each < /ol > tag will turn off the most recent list you started.)
Here's a little example (see Figure 4.4):

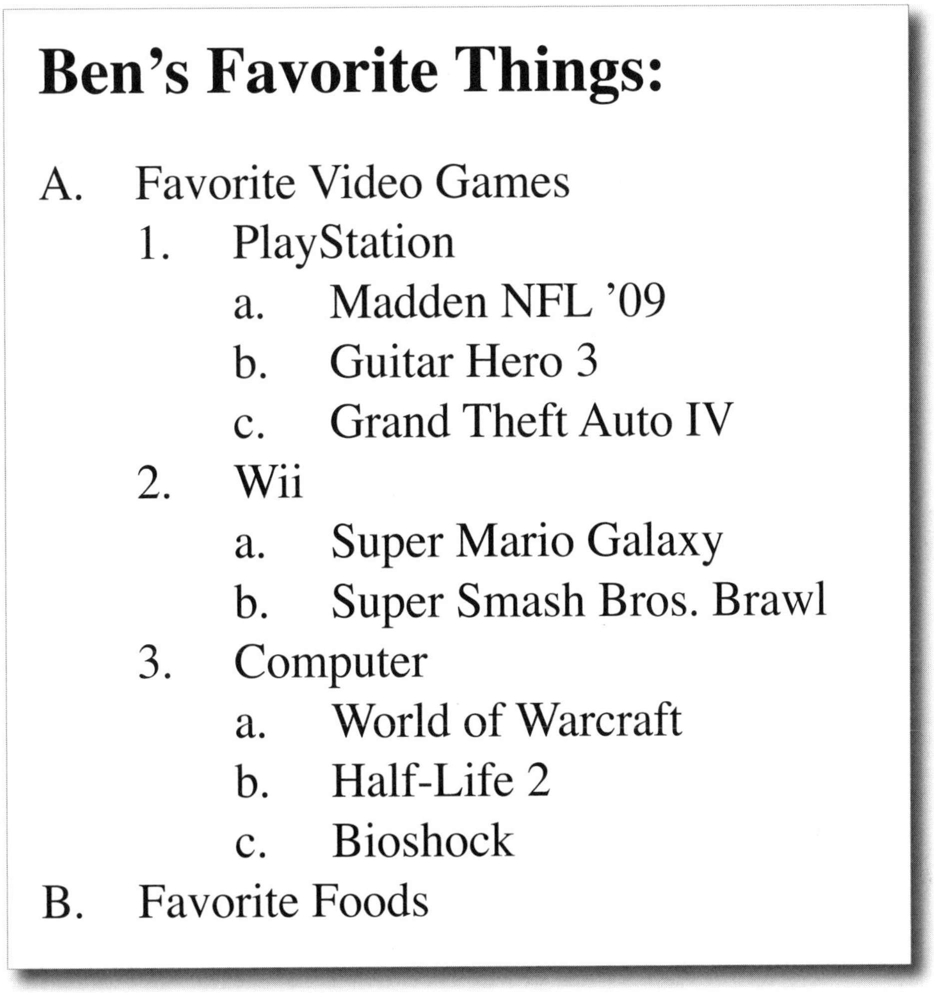

Ben's Favorite Things:

A.   Favorite Video Games
     1.   PlayStation
         a.   Madden NFL '09
         b.   Guitar Hero 3
         c.   Grand Theft Auto IV
     2.   Wii
         a.   Super Mario Galaxy
         b.   Super Smash Bros. Brawl
     3.   Computer
         a.   World of Warcraft
         b.   Half-Life 2
         c.   Bioshock
B.   Favorite Foods

FIGURE 4.4. Using nested ordered lists to create an outline style.

```
<html>
<head>
<title>Ben's favorite things</title>
</head>
<body>
<h3>Ben's favorite things:</h3>
<ol type=A>
<li>Favorite Video Games
```

```
<ol type=1>
<li>PlayStation 3
<ol type=a>
<li>Madden NFL '09
<li>Guitar Hero 3
<li>Grand Theft Auto IV
</ol>
<li>Wii
<ol type=a>
<li>Super Mario Galaxy
<li>Super Smash Bros. Brawl
</ol>
<li>Computer
<ol type=a>
<li>World of Warcraft
<li>Half-Life 2
<li>Bioshock
</ol>
</ol>
<li>Favorite foods
</ol>
</body>
</html>
```

Creating and Using Tables

ⓘ **Did You Know?**

Every time you visit a Web page you can actually see the HTML used to create the page. Go to the "View" menu and select "Source." You'll be amazed at all the stuff you'll see, but you should be able to recognize the tags you know.

Let's go back to the online journal we created in Chapter 2. Remember the list of team players? We listed them in one column down the page. What if we wanted to list them in two columns, to save space on the page and make it look better? If we tried to do this by hand, it would be hard to make the columns line up. An easier and better way is to put the names in a table. Here's the HTML, and Figure 4.5 shows the resulting Web page:

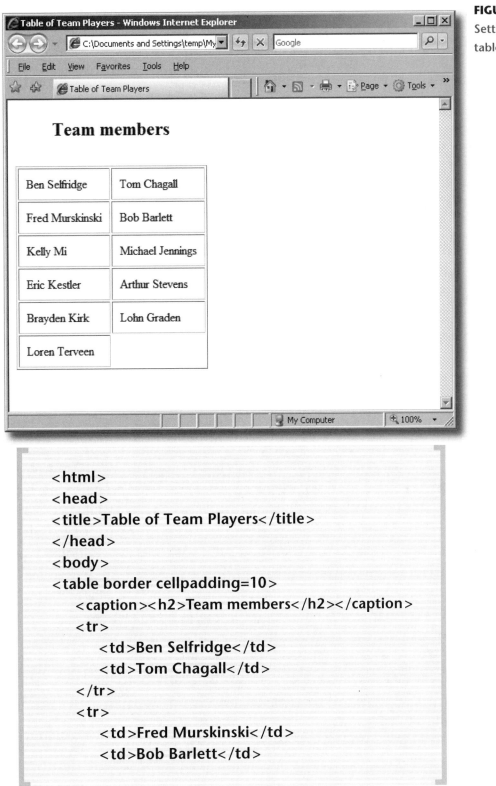

FIGURE 4.5.
Setting up a list in
table form.

```
<html>
<head>
<title>Table of Team Players</title>
</head>
<body>
<table border cellpadding=10>
    <caption><h2>Team members</h2></caption>
    <tr>
        <td>Ben Selfridge</td>
        <td>Tom Chagall</td>
    </tr>
    <tr>
        <td>Fred Murskinski</td>
        <td>Bob Barlett</td>
```

```
        </tr>
        <tr>
            <td>Kelly Mi</td>
            <td>Michael Jennings</td>
        </tr>
        <tr>
            <td>Eric Kestler</td>
            <td>Arthur Stevens</td>
        </tr>
        <tr>
            <td>Brayden Kirk</td>
            <td>Lohn Graden</td>
        </tr>
        <tr>
            <td>Loren Terveen</td>
        </tr>
    </table>
    </body>
    </html>
```

So, what's going on here? Well, we made the list caption ("Team members") a heading because it looks much better that way. We started out with a < **table** > tag with some attributes. (We've talked about adding attributes to tags before; for example, on page 23 we used the < **h1** > tag and added an "align" attribute to center the heading. We also just used the "type" attribute with lists. Go back to page 49 and check it out.) Here we put in the border attribute, which draws lines to separate the cells of the table, and a cellspacing attribute set to 10. This adds more white space around each name so the table doesn't look cramped.

Then, we define each row of the table with the < **tr** > tag, which is easy to remember as "table row." Between each pair of < **tr** > and < /**tr** > tags, we put each table element (or cell) between a < **td** > and < /**td** > tag. We think of < **td** > as standing for "table data."

Let's try one other thing with tables, then you can use the Challenge Questions to explore them yourself. Remember in the last chapter when we put pictures of my dad on a Web page? The caption would start next to the picture, then wrap underneath it, so we put in rules and set up the text as headers. (Go back and look at Figures 3.6 and 3.7 if you want a reminder.) It turns out that you can put an image in a table just as easily as you can text. So, let's use the same HTML code we used in the last example to recreate our page of dad pictures with the images in the lefthand cells and the text we wanted in the righthand cells. That will make the text line up side-by-side with the images the way we wanted. Here's the HTML, and Figure 4.6 shows the resulting Web page:

(i) **Check It Out!**

Poke around on the Web until you find what looks like a list. Look at the source and see if you can find the list tags.

```
<html>
<head>
<title>3Dads</title>
</head>
<body>
<table border>
    <caption><h1>These are three pictures of my
    handsome Dad!</h1></caption>
    <tr>
        <th><img src="images/dad1.gif"></th>
        <th><h2>Here he's about age 45.</h2></th>
    </tr>
    <tr>
        <th><img src="images/dad2.gif"></th>
        <th><h2>Here he's age 48—note the
        disappearing hair and scraggly beard. He blames
        these changes on my becoming a teenager!
</h2></th>
    </tr>
    <tr>
        <th><img src="images/dad3.gif"></th>
```

```
            <th><h2> Here the burden of raising me has
            proved too much and he's become weirded
            out and needs a nap. Ha! Ha!</h2></th>
        </tr>
    </table>
</body>
</html>
```

FIGURE 4.6. Using images and text in a table to make them line up side-by-side.

Here we used an alternative to the table data < **td** > tag. Instead, we used < **th** >, which stands for "table heading." This formats the text as a heading and centers it as well. We think putting the images and text into a table looks much better than what we did in Chapter 3. Also, it really shows how tables can let you put things side by side and then do whatever you want with each side.

Summary

This chapter added to your knowledge of HTML by explaining lists and tables. We showed you how to create a few different kinds of lists, including a nested list that looks like an outline. Then we explored tables by taking part of the journal we created in Chapter 2 and making it into a more compact table. Finally, we put the pictures of my dad into a table so we could put the images and captions side by side.

☞ Challenge Questions

- → Write the table of contents of this book as an HTML list with any style of headings you like.

- → Create a table with three columns instead of two.

- → Reformat your journal from Chapter 2 using lists.

- → Take the table of team members we created in Figure 4.5 and see if you can center it.

- → Take the last table we did, with images and text side by side. See if you can switch the middle picture and its text (so the text is on the left and the image on the right).

5

The Really Fun Stuff:

Using Links to Design a Complete Web Site

Adding Links to Other Pages

FINALLY, we're going to talk about what made the Web what it is today—hypertext links, or links for short. A link is a mouse-sensitive piece of a Web page. (As you'll see, it's usually text but also can be an image or even part of an image.) If clicked on, it will bring up a new Web page in your browser or move the browser to another part of the current Web page.

> ⓘ **Did You Know?**
>
> As of 2007, the Web was estimated to contain more than 19 billion pages (and it's still growing)!

This chapter will:

→ show you how to link one Web page to another page you've created;

→ explain anchors and anchor links that link to different parts of the same Web page;

→ show you how to make a link to any page on the Web;

→ provide examples of image links; and

→ show you how to design and build a complete, multipage Web site.

I'm sure you've heard of a URL, which stands for universal resource locator. A URL is simply the address of a page on the Web (a document, really, but that's not an important distinction right now), like http://www.yahoo.com, http://www.prufrock.com, or http://www.html-for-kids.com. The reason why the Internet is called the World Wide Web is because Web pages have links connecting them to other Web pages, which themselves have links, and so on. So, the entire Web is really a huge, interconnected set of pages. Now let's learn how to put a link into one of your Web pages. First, let's create a new page of links to some of the Web pages you've already made using this book.

Let's say your "My HTML" folder looks like Figure 5.1. (This is what our folder looks like at this point in the book.)

FIGURE 5.1.
Contents of our
"my HTML" file.

Let's create a new Web page that has links to two pages in this folder. We'll start by copying "firstpage.html" and renaming it "mypages.html." (You know how to do this by now.) Then edit the new file in Notepad so it looks like the text below. We are going to examine the new code carefully.

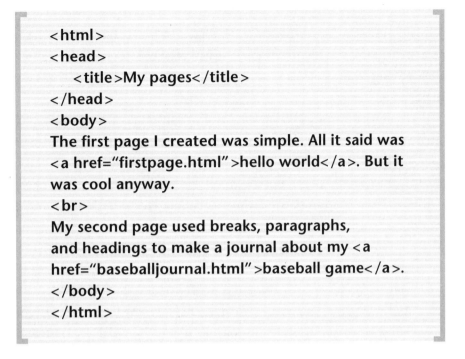

```
<html>
<head>
    <title>My pages</title>
</head>
<body>
The first page I created was simple. All it said was
<a href="firstpage.html">hello world</a>. But it
was cool anyway.
<br>
My second page used breaks, paragraphs,
and headings to make a journal about my <a
href="baseballjournal.html">baseball game</a>.
</body>
</html>
```

Let's look at the most important line in this HTML. It starts with the < a > tag, has a **href=** part (attribute, right?), some text (the "hello world") and then ends with the < /a > tag. The < a > says, essentially, "I want to make a link." The **href=** is then followed by the URL of the link, in this case, "firstpage.html," the page you already made that is in your folder. The text "hello world" forms the link to "firstpage.html."

The link, "hello world," is displayed in the Web page in a special way. In our browser it shows up underlined (and in a different color, but you can't see that here). So, the new page looks like Figure 5.2.

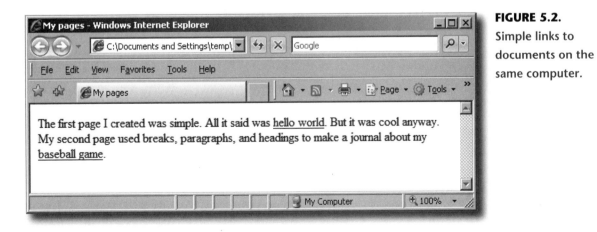

FIGURE 5.2.
Simple links to documents on the same computer.

If you move the mouse over the "Hello world" link, the cursor will turn into a little hand, and if you click on the link, the browser will display your first Web page. Likewise, if you click on "baseball game," you'll get your journal page.

There are two things to note here. First, if you want to display the linked Web page in a new browser window, you can right-click and select "Open Link in New Window." Second, if you don't do this, you will have to use the browser's "Back" button to return to the previous Web page.

The URL we used in this example is called a local URL, meaning it's the address of a Web page on the same machine. When you link to a local URL, you need to specify the path to the file you're linking to. (In this case, because the file is in the same folder, you don't need a path.) But, if the file were in another folder, you'd have to include that folder's name in the path. It turns out you've already done this! In the last chapter, when you put all your images into the "images" folder, then placed an image in your Web page, you used "images/dad1.gif" because the file "dad1.gif" was in the "images" folder.

If you want to add a link to another page on the Web, the command looks exactly the same except for the URL. Here's an example, and Figure 5.3 shows how it looks in your browser.

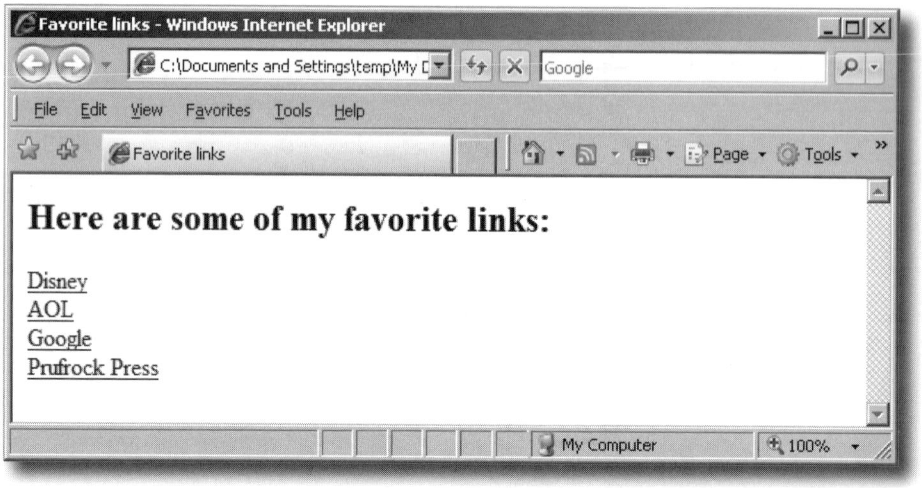

FIGURE 5.3. Links to Web sites.

```
<html>
<head>
<title>Favorite links</title>
</head>

<body>
    <h2>Here are some of my favorite links:</h2>
        <a href="http://www.disney.
        com">Disney</a>
        <br>
        <a href="http://www.aol.com">AOL</a>
        <br>
        <a href="http://www.google.
        com">Google</a>
        <br>
        <a href="http://www.prufrock.com">Prufrock
        Press</a>
<br>
</body>
</html>
```

Adding Image Links

Adding an image link is simple once you know how to add an image and make a link. As an example, I have a Web page named "dadbio.html," which contains a short biography of my dad. I also have an image of my dad called "dad1.html." I can make the image link to the bio page like this:

```
<a href="dadbio.html">
    <img src="images/dad1.gif"><h2>Click the
    image to see my dad's bio</h2></a>
```

FIGURE 5.4.
Examples of image and text links.

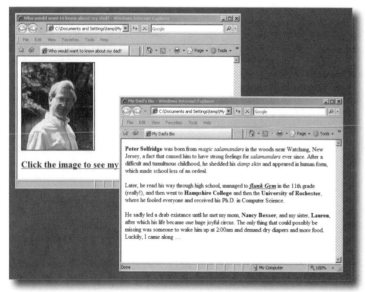

FIGURE 5.5. The linked document opened in a new window.

You see, whatever is after the "< **a href**= . . .>" command becomes the active link. In this case, both the image and the words, "Click the image to see my dad's bio," are links and will bring up the "dadbio.html" page. Figure 5.4 shows how the Web page looks.

We hope you can see that the browser has put a border around the image, indicating that it is a link. (If you don't like the border, you can add the attribute "**border=0**" to the image [< **img** >] tag, and that will get rid of it.) Figure 5.5 shows what you'll get if you click on either the image link or the text. (Here we assume you right-click and select "Open Link in New Window.")

Adding Links to Different Parts of the Same Web Page

Adding links that point to different parts of the same Web page also is easy, but it involves two steps. The first step is to make an anchor in your Web page (we think of it as being like a bookmark) using the name attribute. This attribute names a section, or anchor, so you can put that name into a link.

Because we haven't created a really big Web page yet, we'll just give you a simple example of the idea here. Let's pretend you've expanded your baseball journal (the one you made in Chapter 2) to describe five games you've played. You've chosen to keep all the descriptions on one page. (We'll discuss decisions like this in the next section.) Now you want to add a sort of table of contents to the page, with links so people can go to whichever game they want to read about. What you do is make an anchor at the beginning of each game. Here's what that would look like for a couple of games:

```
<h3><a name="Game 1">Game 1</h3>
<p>
Lots of awesome text describing the game would go
here.
    <h3><a name="Game 2">Game 2</h3>
    <p>
Lots of awesome text describing the game would go
here.
```

What have we done here? It's so easy it's almost silly. We've created a heading for Game 1 and one for Game 2. We named them using the < a > tag and the name attributes "Game 1" and "Game 2." Now, at the top of the page, we can make our table of contents that refers to these anchors with this HTML:

```
<body>
<a name="Top">
<h2>Table of Contents (click to go to each game)
</h2>
    <ol>
        <li><a href="#Game 1">Game 1</a>
        <li><a href="#Game 2">Game 2</a>
    </ol>
```

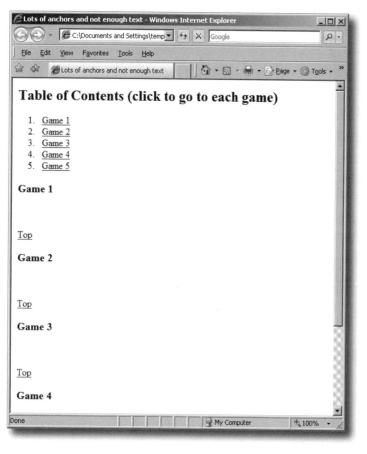

FIGURE 5.6.

Examples of links to navigate down a page and back to the top.

What have we done here? We've made a heading ("Table of Contents") then a basic ordered list. You should remember this from Chapter 4 (see page 49). For each list entry, we've added an < a href= . . .> tag followed by the name of the anchor with a # before it, all in quotation marks. (Why, you ask, does it need a # before it? The answer is we don't know, and you shouldn't care. You just have to use it.)

What this does is to turn each list element into a link to the corresponding anchor. So, if you click on the link, the browser will take you straight to the anchor. Let's take the concept one step further and do what many Web pages do: Add another anchor and link that brings you up to the top of the page again. Here's the framework for five games, and Figure 5.6 shows part of the resulting Web page.

```
<html>
<head>
<title>Lots of anchors and not enough text</title>
</head>
<body>
<a name="Top">
<h2>Table of Contents (click to go to each game)
</h2>
<ol>
    <li><a href="#Game 1">Game 1</a>
    <li><a href="#Game 2">Game 2</a>
```

```
    <li><a href="#Game 3" >Game 3</a>
    <li><a href="#Game 4" >Game 4</a>
    <li><a href="#Game 5" >Game 5</a>
</ol>
<h3><a name="Game 1" >Game 1</h3>
    <br>
    <br>
    <a href="#Top" >Top</a>
<h3><a name="Game 2" >Game 2</h3>
    <br>
    <br>
    <a href="#Top" >Top</a>
<h3><a name="Game 3" >Game 3</h3>
    <br>
    <br>
    <a href="#Top" >Top</a>
<h3><a name="Game 4" >Game 4</h3>
    <br>
    <br>

    <a href="#Top" >Top</a>
<h3><a name="Game 5" >Game 5</h3>
    <br>
    <br>
    <a href="#Top" >Top</a>
</body>
</html>
```

If you look at the links in your browser, you can see they are a different color. If you click on a link in the table of contents, the browser will go to that game. If you click on any of the "Top" links, the browser will go to the top of the page again. We think this is really cool, and so should you!

Did You Know?

Search engines like Google (there are a bunch of others) work by actually creating an *index* of the Web. They do this using computer programs that "crawl" over the Web following all possible links.

Overall Web Site Design

The last (and quite probably the most important) aspect of Web design we need to introduce is making links to your own Web pages. If you've used the Web at all, you are surely aware of how useful these little nuggets of power can be. No detailed Web site can consist of a single page. That means all the pages have to be structured and organized to make it easy for whoever's visiting to navigate your site. Links are the key to making this happen.

Mapping out your Web site is extremely important in making it fun and interesting to visit. It's also one of the most basic processes ever to exist in the computer world. In Figures 5.7 and 5.8, we've given two examples of how to map out a Web site. The arrows represent links from one page to the next, and everything in a rectangle is a page or subpage.

FIGURE 5.7.

Mapping a Web site, Part 1.

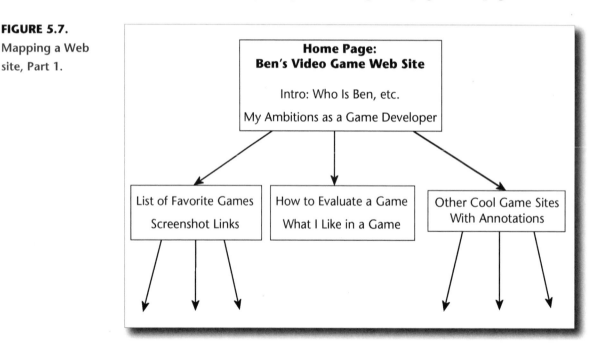

These are two classic designs used all over the place, but you can come up with something original and exciting if you think they're too bland. Maybe you want to have some kind of navigation system on the screen all

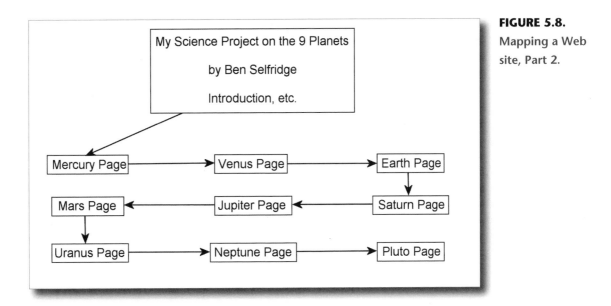

FIGURE 5.8.

Mapping a Web site, Part 2.

the time, such as a bar on the left. Or perhaps you'd prefer to use images as links. Whatever you come up with is great, as long as it works and is not tedious to the person who's visiting.

Once you've developed a map of what you want on the pages and how they're linked, the next step is to design each page. Depending on the purpose of your Web site, you may want each page to have a similar style, or as is sometimes said, a similar "look and feel." The reason for a consistent design is to give your visitors an intuitive sense of where they are. Of course, this is easier said than done unless you're a professional Web designer. But, you can take some simple steps that will help:

→ Select a nice background color and use it on all of your pages.

→ Select a nice and readable font (and a color that goes with the background) and use that for most, if not all, of your text.

→ Lay out each page so that it is simple to view: not too crowded, and obvious in its intent.

These simple guidelines will go a long way toward making a pleasing Web site.

Building a Web Site From Several Pages

So, let's actually build a Web site from some of the pages we've created. Let's say the purpose of the Web site is to show someone the work that you've done, or maybe this is just part of your personal Web site.

Let's take the folder of pages we showed in Figure 5.1 and use that directly in our design. The folder we showed actually had the Web pages in three handy rows more or less corresponding to the Web pages we developed during Chapter 2 (Fun With Fonts), Chapter 3 (Interesting Images), and Chapter 4 (Likeable Lists and Terrific Tables). So, let's imagine a main page with links to each of these pages, as in Figure 5.9.

FIGURE 5.9.

Graphic showing links from a main page to all of the Web pages we've created.

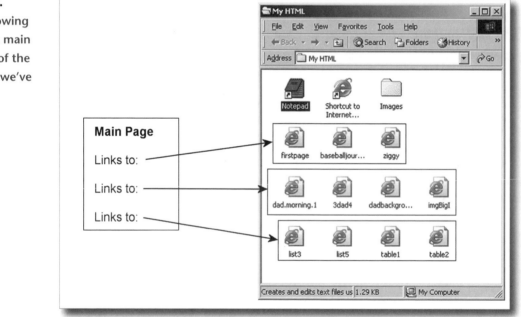

So, how do we want the main page to look? Let's sketch out a rough design, shown in Figure 5.10.

What will the HTML look like? Well, we're really hoping that by now you could do this yourself! And we bet you can! Here are a few tips, then we'll do the actual link section as a table:

→ The title will be a level 1 heading (you remember, < **h1** >).

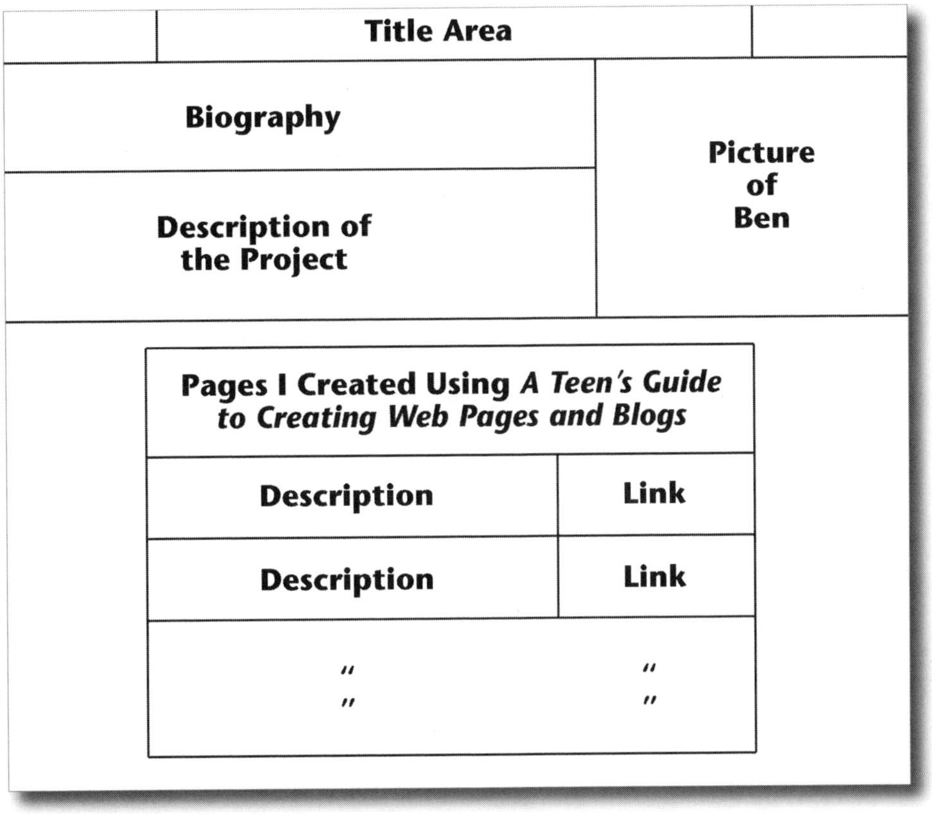

FIGURE 5.10.
Rough design of
the main page.

	Title Area	
Biography		**Picture of Ben**
Description of the Project		

Pages I Created Using *A Teen's Guide to Creating Web Pages and Blogs*	
Description	Link
Description	Link
" "	" "

→ The biography, description, and picture will be a table with one row and two columns, and the second column will have an image in it.

→ The links will be in a table with three rows and multiple columns.

So, how are we going to set up the table of links? Well, let's use lists in the second column of each table row, and each list will be a list of links to the pages you've created. Indenting your HTML really helps here.

```
<table border cellpadding=5>
<caption><h2>Web Pages I Created Using<i>A
Teen's Guide to Creating Web Pages and
Blogs</i></h2></caption>
<tr>
```

```
    <td>Mainly Text Pages</td>
    <td>
        <ol>
            <li><a href="firstpage.html">Hello
            World</a>
            <li><a href="baseballjournal.html">
            Baseball Journal</a>

            <li><a href="ziggy.html">Ziggy in a
            Different Font</a>
        </ol>
    </td>
</tr>
<tr>
    <td>Pages With Images in Them</td>
    <td>
        <ol>
            <li><a href="dad.morning1.html">My
            Dad in the Morning</a>
            <li><a href="3dad4.html">Three More
            Pictures of My Dad.</a>
            <li><a href="dadbackground.
            html"><b>Don't look at this!</b></a>
        </ol>
    </td>
</tr>
<tr>
    <td>Pages With Lists and Tables</td>
    <td>
        <ol>
            <li><a href="list3.html">My Favorite
            Foods</a>
            <li><a href="list5.html">Other Favorite
            Things</a>
            <li><a href="table1.html">Baseball
            Players in a Table</a>
```

```
<li><a href="table2.html" >My Dad's
Pictures in a Table</a>
</ol>
</td>
</table>
```

Figure 5.11 shows how it looks. Each list item on the right is a link to a page you created. Isn't this cool?

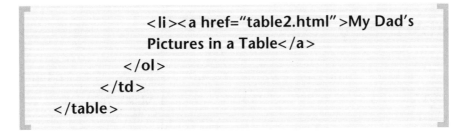

FIGURE 5.11.
Links set up in table format.

Web Pages I Created Using *A Teen's Guide to Creating Web Pages and Blogs*

Mainly Text Pages	1. Hello World 2. Baseball Journal 3. Ziggy in a Different Font
Pages With Images in Them	1. My Dad in the Morning 2. Three More Pictures of My Dad 3. **Don't Look at This!**
Pages With Lists and Tables	1. My Favorite Foods 2. Other Favorite Things 3. Baseball Players in a Table 4. My Dad's Pictures in a Table

Summary

We started this chapter with a brief discussion of URLs and links, making a simple page that linked to two other pages we'd already made and stored on our computer. Then, we made some links to Web sites on the Internet and showed you how to make an image into a link. (How cool is that?) Making links from one section to another of the same page is pretty easy too: all you have to do is to define anchors and use the anchors in your < **href** > tag. Then we switched gears a bit and talked about different ways to organize a Web site and design a Web page. Finally, we made a page that put links inside a table.

☞ Challenge Questions

→ What happens if you click on a link that doesn't point to a valid Web page? Has that ever happened to you before?

→ Go to a Web page you're familiar with and look at the source. Can you find the links in the source?

→ Use the example in Figure 5.11, but see if you can make the links in a nested table (that is, a table within the cell of another table) inside the righthand table cells. This looks pretty neat.

6

Publishing Your Work on the Web:

Showing the World What You Can Do

Introduction

HEY, fooling around learning HTML on your computer is fine, but if you actually want other people to see your work, you have to publish it. By publish it, we mean putting it on a Web server on the Internet. So, we're going to take this opportunity to tell you a bit about how the Web works. (Just a little bit, so don't worry!)

The Web, or Internet, is a network of computers linked together. Some computers are Web servers, which means they can provide Web pages to other computers hooked up to the Internet. Each Web server has an address called an Internet protocol (IP) address, which is a 12-digit number written like this: 123.987.456.654. Luckily, you don't have to remember any IP addresses because there's a way of mapping URLs to their IP addresses. This means you and your computer

This chapter will:

→ explain a little bit how the entire Web works;

→ suggest a way to organize and check your work before you publish it on the Web;

→ show you some places where you can publish your Web site; and

→ describe how to register your own domain name if you get really serious!

can use http://www.prufrock.com instead of the site's 12-digit number. (Of course, if you knew the 12-digit number was 69.49.170.18, you could actually type that into your browser.)

When you start your browser and type in a URL, your computer sends a message over the Internet to the Web server that corresponds to that URL. (The protocol, or "language," it uses is called HTTP, which stands for Hypertext Transfer Protocol. This is why URLs start with "http://", although you can almost always leave that off now.) If you click on a link, the computer usually sends a message with a URL followed by some other information that tells the Web server what page you want. The Web server then finds the page you requested and sends it back to your computer, and your browser then displays it. That's pretty much all there is to it!

Organizing and Checking Your Work

The first step toward publishing your HTML on a Web site is to create your Web pages on your computer. You can do that with what you've learned in this book. In this book, we've also shown you a couple of ways to organize Web pages, as well as how to put things like images into their own separate folders and, in general, keep everything as organized as possible. The bottom line is to make sure everything works exactly the way you want it to on your computer. Only when you are sure you've worked the bugs out should you plan on publishing your pages to a Web site.

Steps in Publishing Your Web Pages

Lots of Web hosting companies will allow you to publish your Web pages on their Web server for free (at least if the pages are not too large), and we recommend this as a first step. Unfortunately, they do insist on putting advertisements on your page, but hey, they have to make money somehow! We aren't going to recommend a particular site, because it might be out-of-date by the time you read this book. Instead, we suggest you go to Google or another search engine and type in "free Web site" or something like that. You should have no problem finding a place to publish your work. You also can purchase your own domain name (see below).

Once you've made sure everything works on your computer and have picked a place to publish your Web site, the rest is easy. Basically, all you need to do is to follow their directions to upload your files (all of the HTML files you've built, including directories or folders that hold images).

There's one thing we didn't tell you yet that may be important. There's a convention that your home page, the first page displayed when people visit your site, is called "index.html." We're not sure why that is, but if you put your stuff on the Web, you may have to rename your home page. No big deal, obviously.

Once you've loaded your stuff on the Web, you'll want to follow every link and visit every page to make sure everything works right. Again, if you've already checked everything once on your computer, this step should be easy.

Domain Names

You may already know this, but you can register your own domain name (http://www.yourname.com), as long as the name is not already taken. Once you've registered a domain name, you "own" it for a period of time (such as a year). Registering costs a modest fee (well, depending on how much money you have), depending on the site you use. One, GoDaddy.com, is really easy to use and only costs $9.99 a year. This site allows you to look up domain names to find out if anyone has the one you want. We registered http://www.html-for-kids.com for this book, and the process was really pretty easy. The outfit that registers your domain name for you also will be very happy to host your Web site (although not for free) and sell you additional services such as e-mail and stuff like that. Sometimes, services that come with your computer, such as Apple's MobileMe program, which you can opt to pay for when you purchase a Macintosh computer or a device compatible with the program, will host your site for free as part of your membership fee (which also includes e-mail, instant messaging, and other cool tools).

Summary

This chapter briefly explained how to take the HTML Web pages you developed on your own computer and put them on the Web using a Web hosting company. Many companies will host your site for free but will put advertisements into your Web page. Before publishing, the most important thing to remember is to check your work carefully and completely understand what you've done. If you've done this, uploading your files so they appear correctly on the Web should be pretty straightforward.

☞ Challenge Questions

→ See if your name is registered as a domain name. First try to go to http://www.yourname.com and see what happens. If you don't reach a Web site, go to a site that allows you to register domain names and see if your name is available.

→ Use the Web pages you've built using this book to design your own Web site. First, sketch out your site as we've shown you, then actually build it!

→ Publish your pages on the Web. Tell your friends!

7

A Little Bit of JavaScript:
The Power of Programming

Jump Right in With Alerts

LET'S jump right in with a simple example of JavaScript. Create a file called JavaScript1.html with the following HTML in it:

```html
<html>
<head>
    <title>My first little JavaScript
    </title>
    <script language="javascript">
        alert ("Are you aware that you
        are visiting the Web site of a
        very cool person?");
        alert ("Well, now you know!")
    </script>
</head>
```

This chapter will:

→ show you a very easy and cool addition to a Web page called an alert;

→ explain a little bit about JavaScript, which is a real programming language;

→ show you some neat things you can do with JavaScript; and

→ we hope, get you interested enough to start learning JavaScript on your own!

```
<body>
<p>
<h1>I'm sure glad we got that out of the way!<h1>
</body>
</html>
```

Now run the file in your browser and see what happens. You should get two alerts, one after the other. The first will say, "Are you aware that you are visiting the Web site of a very cool person?" and the second, "Well, now you know!" Each will stay up until you click the "OK" button. Then, when you click the second "OK," the Web page will open with "I'm sure glad we got that out of the way!" as a heading. Figure 7.1 shows what the first alert looks like:

FIGURE 7.1.
Example of an alert.

Pretty cool, huh?

ⓘ Did You Know?

Have you heard of Java as well as JavaScript? Believe it or not, Java and JavaScript have *nothing* to do with each other. Why they have the same name is a mystery to us.

JavaScript: What's It About?

JavaScript is a computer language that allows you to write computer programs that run as part of your Web page. HTML is a computer language, too. But, as you now know, it is pretty much limited to describing how a Web page looks. JavaScript can do much, much more. One way it often is used is to check data entered into a Web page. (We're going to do that in the next JavaScript example.) But it also can do almost any kind of computation there is. It really is a general-purpose computer language.

Unfortunately, we're not going to talk much about JavaScript, only show you some tricks you can use to make your Web page more fun. Learning JavaScript is a great idea, and we really recommend it. Just like with HTML, the best way to learn JavaScript is to get a book, sit down at the computer, and do it.

So, let's go back to the example we just gave. What's going on here? Let's repeat the important lines:

```
<script language="javascript">
    alert ("Are you aware that you are visiting the
    Web site of a very cool person?");
    alert ("Well, now you know!")
</script>
```

First, we used the < script > tag to start a script section, and we specified that we were going to use JavaScript as our language. Then we put in two JavaScript alert commands. Because you ran your JavaScript1. html in your browser, you should have a really good idea what an alert command does. Basically, it pops up a little text box with a message in it. Further, it pretty much forces you to read the message because nothing else will happen until you hit the "OK" button. In this case, after you click "OK" on the first alert, a second alert pops up. Only after that is accepted is the rest of the Web page displayed. Alerts are kind of fun, but they're also pretty intrusive. If you put those two alerts inside a Web page you wanted people to visit often, you'd be surprised (or maybe you wouldn't) how quickly people would get tired of them. For this reason, use alerts sparingly and for good reasons. What might a good reason be? Check out the next example.

Entering and Checking Input to a Web Page

You know, so far all we have shown you is how to display information in a Web page. But you know from using the Web yourself that you are often asked to enter information. How is this done? Rather than talk about it abstractly, let's look at an example:

```html
<html>
<head>
    <title>My second little JavaScript</title>
    <script language=javascript>
        function CheckForReasonableAge() {
            age = window.prompt ("How old are
            you?")
            if (age == 16)
                alert ("Wow! How cool is that! That's my
                age!")
            else
            if (age < 5)
                alert ("That's too young! I don't believe
                you!");
            else
            if (age > 95)
                alert ("That's too old! I don't believe
                you!")
            else
                alert ("Hmmm. OK. I guess that's
                interesting.")
        }
    </script>
</head>
<body>
    <INPUT TYPE=button value="Click on this"
```

```
            onClick="CheckForReasonableAge()" >
        </body>
    </html>
```

Don't freak out! It's not that complicated! We'll explain every piece of this. But before we do, why don't you enter it into a file called "JavaScript2.html" and try running it in your browser? You should get a Web page with a button, and if you click on it, a little form should pop up that looks like Figure 7.2 (my dad actually entered his age into the form).

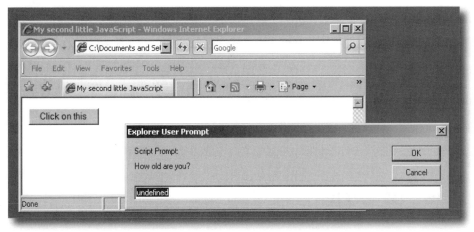

FIGURE 7.2.
Entering information into a Web page.

Now try entering different numbers in the little box and hitting "Enter" Try the numbers -55, 3, 5, 13, your age, and 111111. Then look back at the Java-Script code. You'll probably begin to get the idea what this code does right away. But "getting the idea" is not enough. Let's really try to understand the code. There are two obvious parts, the script part and the body. Let's look at the body first.

The body starts with an < **INPUT** > tag with three attributes, one of which is special. < **INPUT** > means that the Web page is going to ask the user for some input (duh!). The attribute "Type" specifies that the input is going to be a button and the value is simply the label that appears on the button. Then comes the special attribute. What this says is simply, "When the button is clicked, 'call' or 'go to' the function 'CheckForReasonable-Age.'" This means that the Web page starts to execute, or run, the code called "CheckForReasonableAge" in the script part of the page.

The script part describes what is called a *function*, and the name of the function is "CheckForReasonableAge." A function is simply some code that does not run automatically (as the alerts did) but has to be called using its name. We'll explain more about this in just a minute.

So, when you enter an age into the form and hit "Enter," the CheckForReasonableAge function is called and is "given" the form. The CheckForReasonableAge function gets the actual age you typed using the 'age = window.prompt ("How old are you?")' statement and uses that to do three comparisons. If you read == as "is equal to," < as "is less than," and > as "is greater than," you should be able to understand the code.

This is an odd example—probably not something anyone would want to do. But how might you use this type of code? Well, have you ever had to register for something and enter your email address on a Web page? You might have noticed that if you enter your address incorrectly (without an @, for example) the Web page will complain (often with an alert). This is almost certainly done with JavaScript.

List of Squares

JavaScript is much more powerful than these examples—in fact, it's a real programming language with variables and loops. Here's one more simple example:

```
<html>
<head>
<title>for loops</title>
<script language="JavaScript">
    for (i = 1; i <= 25; i++) {
        j = i*i
        document.write (i + " squared is: " + j +
        "<br>")
    }
```

```
</script>
</head>
</html>
```

Type this code into a file named JavaScript2.html, and give it a try. You should get Figure 7.3.

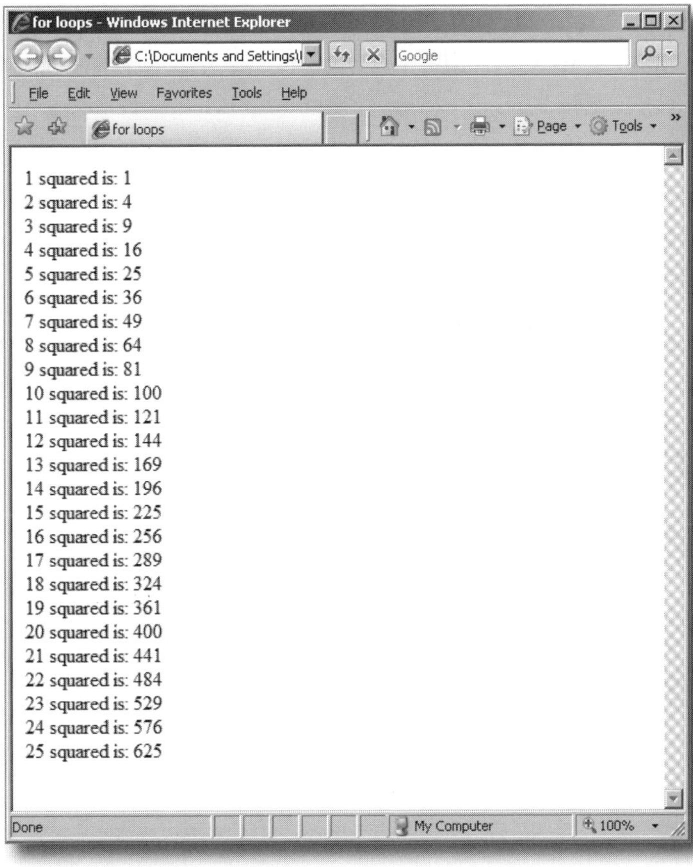

```
1 squared is: 1
2 squared is: 4
3 squared is: 9
4 squared is: 16
5 squared is: 25
6 squared is: 36
7 squared is: 49
8 squared is: 64
9 squared is: 81
10 squared is: 100
11 squared is: 121
12 squared is: 144
13 squared is: 169
14 squared is: 196
15 squared is: 225
16 squared is: 256
17 squared is: 289
18 squared is: 324
19 squared is: 361
20 squared is: 400
21 squared is: 441
22 squared is: 484
23 squared is: 529
24 squared is: 576
25 squared is: 625
```

FIGURE 7.3.
A function for finding mathematical squares written using JavaScript.

So, what's happening here? The first new idea here is that of a variable. Here, this JavaScript uses two variables: i and j. You can think of a variable as a little envelope that can hold a value. In particular, envelope j is set equal to i*i, which means "i times i," or i squared. (We actually used a variable called "age" in the last example.)

The second new idea is that of a loop. A loop is a way of running a bunch of JavaScript commands again and again. We've used a for loop, which is probably the most popular kind. The for loop uses another variable called i, and here's what it does. First, it sets i equal to 1—that's the "i=1" part. Then it checks to make sure that i is less than or equal to 25. If it isn't (that is, if i is 26 or higher), it stops the loop. If it is (which it will be for a while, especially because we've just set i equal to 1), it executes what is between the curly brackets { }. Then it adds 1 to i—that's the "i++" part. (The "++" is called an operator because it operates on the variable i by adding 1 to it.) Does this make sense? Finally, it shouldn't surprise you that "document. write" writes to the Web page, and can write both text (what is between the quotation marks) and the value of a variable. So, instead of writing i on the page, it writes i's value. If you look at the code carefully, then look at the output, you should figure out the gist of this. See the Challenge Questions to test yourself.

Summary

This chapter has shown you a little bit of JavaScript. Unlike in previous chapters, we don't really expect you to do much more than study the code and our explanations and understand them as best you can. You probably won't be able to write much original JavaScript on your own at this point. Of course, feel free to experiment as much as you like.

☞ Challenge Questions

→ Try making your own alerts. They are fun.

→ Change the JavaScript program we showed you so that it prints out not only the squares of the numbers from 1 to 25, but also their cubes.

8

What's Next?

Introduction

THERE is so much more you can do with HTML, and learning HTML leads you to learn many other fun things as well. So we'll have to restrain ourselves. We'll just briefly talk about style sheets, which are really important. Then we'll tell you some other nifty things about HTML and a few other cool Web technologies, some of which I have been playing around with.

In this chapter, you'll see several exciting things, including a little about cascading style sheets (or CSS, for short) and other HTML things that are a little more advanced. Now, because this book is specifically a tutorial introduction to HTML, we (unfortunately) cannot go into very much depth. Please enjoy this chapter! We hope it will tickle your fancy enough to make you pursue more knowledge (perhaps in a future book by us).

This chapter will:

→ briefly describe a few other cool things you can look forward to learning about if the stuff in this book grabs you.

Cascading Style Sheets and DHTML

Although HTML is fun to play around with and is useful for creating Web pages, it's not exactly versatile. That is, it often is frustrating because it won't do what you want in terms of positioning items on the screen, choosing font color, and many other features. Meet CSS. CSS is kind of complicated, so we're just going to mention it. This amazingly nifty tool allows Web designers (that's you) to define the color, position, font type, and everything (yes, everything) else you could possibly want for a text or image.

CSS can do two different things:

1. It can allow you to redefine a tag, such as < h1 >, to do something else. (For instance, it could make the text between the tags red or really big.)
2. It can allow you to define whole new sets of properties that you can use later in your HTML.

In fact, if you combine CSS with JavaScript (that mutant language featured in Chapter 7) and something called the Document Object Model (DOM), you get what is called Dynamic HTML (DHTML). Again, that's another acronym that sounds really complicated, but in fact, it isn't. (We've always thought that the computer world sounded too complicated for its own good.) With this ingenious system and a good understanding of JavaScript and CSS, you can change and animate objects on the screen.

Frames

Have you ever seen a Web page that was divided into different sections? These might include a navigation bar on the left, a title at the top that is separated from the rest of the page, and the content in the middle section. All of these sections are called *frames*. Each one is actually a separate Web page, merged in the final frameset (basically all of the pages put together, which is what the visitor sees). In fact, if you select "View" on the bar at the top of your screen, then select "Source" or "View Source" to see the HTML code behind the page, you will see something like this:

```
<html>
<head>
    <title>Some Sort of Title</title>
</head>
<body>
    <frameset cols="110,*,110">
    <frame src="nav.html" name="1navigation">
    <frame src="content.html" name="content">
    <frame src="photos.html" name="pictures">
</body>
</html>
```

Here, the sources for all the different frames are "**nav.html**," "**content.html**," and "**photos.html**." Now, we're going to do something cool with this information. See the text box at the top, by the other options, that contains the URL of the page? Highlight everything after the very last "/" in it.

Delete this part, then type in "**nav.html**," or one of the other pages you saw in the source of the original page. Press "Enter," and you will see that frame standing by itself in the screen! Some pages have JavaScript that will protect you from seeing one frame by itself, but many coders overlook that step, allowing you to see in turn the code they used to make each frame!

Other Cool Web Technologies and Applications

We'd like just to mention some other cool Web technologies and applications that you might be interested in learning about:

→ **Flash:** Flash is a system for creating and displaying animations on the Web. A company called Macromedia created it. If you've ever seen cartoon-like animations on the Web, they were probably created using Flash.

→ **IM:** IM stands for "Instant Messenger," and we'd be really surprised if you haven't heard of it—in fact, you probably use it! This nifty application lets you "chat" with your friends and other people on the Web, send files and other kinds of information, and keep handy buddy lists. It will even tell you when a buddy is logged on and can be contacted.

→ **Java:** Java is a full-fledged programming language that is more complicated than JavaScript and is used to create Web content. You use Java to create what is called a Java Applet that can run in your browser.

→ **XML:** XML is supposed to be a replacement for HTML, but it doesn't seem to have caught on as fast as people expected it to. XML allows you to create your own tags and define what you want those tags to mean.

Other Ways to Create Web Sites

We hope you've enjoyed your tutorial on building Web sites from scratch, and we certainly hope that you will use it to make your own site. However, being a teen, I know that teens are busy and you might not have the time right now to make your own Web site, but you still want a presence on the Web. The next two chapters will help you do just that!

☞ Challenge Questions

→ The only challenge question for this chapter is: Have fun experimenting with the Web!

Meeting and Greeting on the Web:

9

Building Great Pages on Social Networking Sites (SNS)

Principal Social Networking Sites

ODDS are, you probably already know what social networking sites are, even if you haven't heard them called that. The simplest definition of a social networking site (SNS) is a Web site that allows registered users to make a public or semi-public profile (the "social" part) and link that profile to other people's profiles (the "network" part). Basically, when you register on an SNS and start adding friends, your friends become part of your big social web, and you can view all of the connections between yourself and them. The two most popular SNSs in North America are MySpace and Facebook, and you might already use them to keep in touch with your friends, post photos or videos, or join groups

This chapter will:

→ discuss the many different types of social networking sites;

→ show you how to create MySpace, Facebook, and Flickr profiles;

→ give detailed advice on customizing your MySpace page using both html and predesigned templates;

→ help you personalize your Facebook homepage; and

→ teach you how to organize and share your photos on the Web using Flickr.

of people who share your interests. There are hundreds of SNSs out there and an endless amount of cool things you can do on them, but some of them are designed more for teens and teen interests. Besides MySpace and Facebook, which we'll come back to later, other big networking sites include Bebo (http://www.bebo.com), Friendster (http://www.friendster.com), and Habbo (http://www.habbo.com).

Bebo was launched in 2005 (Garfield, 2006) and is pretty similar to Facebook, letting you add different skins and applications to really reflect your personality. You can leave notes on your friends' walls or draw on their White Board, you can add music videos to your profile, upload your photos, join groups, and much more. One really cool thing about Bebo is that it's a great place to find pen pals in other countries, because it's popular in places like Great Britain and Ireland, as well as the United States. If you decide to sign up on Bebo, you'll notice that they recommend setting your profile to private if you are under 18. That way only your friends will be able to see your information. Even then, you should be extra careful about the information you put on your profile (make sure to read the cybersafety chapter of this book—it will give you important rules for protecting yourself online).

Friendster took off in 2003 (Inoue, 2003) and is popular in the US along with a several Asian countries (ComScore.com, 2007). One cool thing about Friendster is that it was one of the first sites to let users see their Circle of Friends. Your Circle of Friends isn't just your friends, but all of your friends' friends too. The Circle of Friends has gotten more advanced over the years, and now you can see the series of relationships that connect you to anyone in your network. As simple as it sounds, a few years ago it was a revolution! Making friends with your friends' friends is one of the best and safest ways to gain buddies on an SNS. And, even if you don't have a ton of friends on Friendster, it's still a neat site to explore. It has a lot of the same features as Bebo and Facebook, including custom privacy controls.

Habbo is a really different site, but it's still tons of fun. Unlike the other SNSs, Habbo was made specifically for kids and teens. On Habbo you get to make an avatar—a graphic version of yourself—and interact with other avatars called Habbos in different rooms of the Habbo Hotel. You can always enter the Habbo Hotel by clicking on the green button in the upper righthand corner of your homepage. Your homepage is your starting point and the first page you'll see once you register on Habbo. Figure 9.1 shows what it looks like.

FIGURE 9.1. A screen shot of Habbo's interface.

From your homepage you can edit your profile page (under the "My Page" tab), change your account settings, play games, and explore the Habbo community! Just remember that the Habbo Hotel is where everyone hangs out. Once you pick a room in the hotel to explore—like the Flava Burger Bar or the Library of Alexandria—you can move around and chat with other Habbos (see Figure 9.2), instant message them, and view their profile pages, where they can tell you a little about themselves.

The Habbo Hotel isn't all public chat rooms. Every Habbo has its own private hotel room that you get to decorate with awesome furniture and accessories. But unfortunately, buying things for your room on Habbo means you have to have Habbo coins, which cost real money. Habbo coins

FIGURE 9.2. An example of a public chat room in the Habbo Hotel.

can be bought online, over the phone, or by mail, but always check with your parents before purchasing anything online!

It's important to know that Facebook, Bebo, and Habbo only allow users who are at least 13 years old to register, MySpace only allows users who are 14 and older to register, and Friendster only allows members who are 16 and older.

MySpace

Most people have heard of MySpace, even if they don't use it—it's definitely the most popular SNS, for a lot of good reasons! MySpace launched in 2003, but at the time it wasn't much more than a copycat site of Friendster, because some of the people who worked at Friendster decided to create

MySpace (Greenspan, 2006). 2004 was "the year of MySpace," when the site really started to explode with the public. As MySpace's popularity grew, it began to add more and more features; until it eventually became the communications giant we know and love today. But, like every SNS, MySpace's main feature is the profile pages it allows its users to create. The starting point of your MySpace profile is your homepage. A link to your homepage is always located on the left side of a menu bar at the top of your screen. This menu is generally in the same place on most MySpace pages, so if you ever get lost, you can always find your way back to your homepage. Your homepage is where you can check your messages, write and manage your blogs, edit your friends list, approve and deny friend requests, read and post bulletins (which will pop up on your friends' homepages, just like a big bulletin board), plus edit and manage most of the information on your profile (including pictures). Basically, your homepage is where you make things happen! When you first sign up for MySpace, you'll want to spend some time familiarizing yourself with the things on your homepage. It'll come in handy later on, when you really get into using MySpace.

Once you're on your homepage, try playing around with some of the features—just for fun. Find the "MySpace Links" box and try clicking on the first link, "Apps" (see Figure 9.3). "Apps" is short for applications, which are fun little programs you can add to your page to spice things up. Click on "Animals and Pets," and you'll get a whole list of applications you can add to your profile if they look cool to you. There are a ton of options— everything from a virtual pet cat to a quiz designed to tell you what kind of puppy you are! Have fun playing with the apps, but remember that a whole bunch of apps can clutter up a profile page pretty fast.

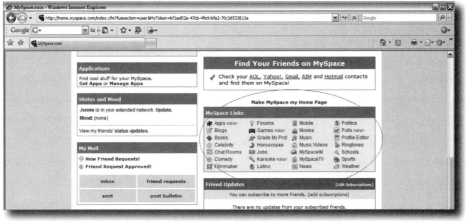

FIGURE 9.3.
MySpace links.

Back on your homepage, you'll find links to other MySpace features you'll definitely want to explore. Some of my favorites are MySpace Karaoke, where you can record yourself singing your favorite songs (as long as you have a microphone) and post them to your profile; MySpace Movies, where you can watch trailers and get info on all the hottest movies; and MySpace TV, where you can watch funny or amazing videos. With MySpace IM, you can instant message your friends that are logged onto MySpace at the same time you are, and on MySpace News, you can submit the news stories that you think are important. MySpace users will rate these news stories, and the higher the rating a story gets, the further it will move up the news page. MySpace also has a neat classifieds section where you can buy, sell, and trade things like textbooks and CD's.

FIGURE 9.4.

MySpace "Add/ Edit Photos" link.

One of the very first things you'll want to do on your homepage, however, is search for friends you already know. On your homepage, you'll see a box above the MySpace Links box with a headline that says "Find Your Friends on MySpace." Using this feature you can automatically find your friends through your e-mail and chat programs. Or, you can go back to that main menu bar at the top of every MySpace page, click the "Search" link, and find people by name that might not be on your e-mail or chat programs. This is a really great way to find people that you've lost track of or haven't seen in awhile, like friends from summer camp.

One of MySpace's most popular features is the photo album. From your homepage, find the link that says "Add/ Edit Photos," up by your default picture (see Figure 9.4). Click on that link, and you'll come to a screen where you can start uploading your photos. See the menu bar at the top of the page? Try clicking on "Create Album," then give your new album a name, like "My Family." You'll also need to choose whether this album is private (viewable by only you); viewable by your MySpace friends only; or viewable by everyone on the Internet. Most of the time, it's a good idea to make your photos viewable by friends only, but if you have an album of family vacation pictures, you might want to make it viewable by everyone so you can send the link to other family members. Just be aware of who is able to view your pictures.

Once you've created your album, you'll be taken back to the main photo page, where your new album will appear as empty. You then can click on the "Upload Photos" link at the top left of your page, and click "Browse" to find the photos on your computer that you'd like to add to the album. Click next, then select the name of the new album from the drop-down album list and click "Upload." Once you're done uploading the picture, click next again, and you'll be given a chance to "tag" people in the picture—basically, create a link in the picture to that person's MySpace profile—or add a caption to the picture. You can create as many albums as you'd like and upload an unlimited amount of pictures. And you can always come back to your "My Albums" page to create more albums, add or delete photos, tag your friends in photos, and make slideshows (see Figure 9.5).

FIGURE 9.5. Photo album display on MySpace.

Once you're familiar with your homepage, you'll want to really get into creating your profile. Most MySpace profiles share some common features that you should know about. At the very top of your profile on the right side will be a box with links to your blog entries, if you choose to keep a blog on MySpace. There's a standard About Me section where you can tell the world a little about yourself. There's also an I'd Like to Meet . . . blurb where you can let your site visitors know the kind of people you might like to be MySpace buddies with. Below that is a box with your Top 8 friends (which you designate on your homepage) and under that, your comments section, where your friends can leave you text or picture comments that are displayed on your profile.

On the top left side of your profile is your default picture, which you can upload in the Add/Edit Photos section. Your default picture is the picture that will be displayed next to your comments on your friends' pages; it also will pop up if someone searches for you by name. Basically, this is a public picture even if your profile is marked private, so make sure it's a picture you wouldn't be hesitant to show your parents or class-mates! Beneath your default picture you'll find a contact box, where visi-tors on your page can click to send you messages, add you as a friend, and a few other things. Just below your contact box is a box containing your MySpace URL, which is a unique location that you pick when you first sign up for MySpace. You can always change your display name, but you cannot change your MySpace URL, which is the address people will type in to visit your page, so make sure it's something you can live with. Figure 9.6 shows what a typical MySpace profile will look like.

One of the most unique MySpace features is that it allows users to add HTML or CSS to their profile in order to completely change the look and feel of the page (and now you know HTML, so you're all set!). There are some reasons to both love this feature and to hate it. The best part is, of course, that you can completely control the look of your profile. You can change your background to a graphic of your choosing or customize your contact table. You can change your Top 8 to include as many friends as you'd like. Basically, you can pretty much do whatever your HTML skills allow. On the other hand, this means that some people will go completely overboard. We've all visited MySpace profiles where all the crazy back-grounds, blinking graphics, and translucent boxes made things really annoying and difficult to read!

FIGURE 9.6. A typical MySpace profile.

The HTML or CSS code that goes into creating a cool MySpace profile can be somewhat complicated, but fortunately there are plenty of sites out there that can help. Some of the most popular sites offer predesigned profile pages—all you have to do is copy and paste the code into your profile, and it will give your page a whole new look. Let's play around with one of these predesigned layouts. My favorite site to find them is Pyzam (http://www.pyzam.com). Head over there and click on the "Myspace Layouts" section on the lefthand side of the screen, then browse through the hundreds of neat layouts.

When you find one that you like, click on the picture of it to go to a page where you can preview it full-screen and get the code. I found one I liked called "Bloom," so I decided to get the code to make it my layout (see Figure 9.7). All I have to do to turn my layout into the Bloom layout is copy the code given to me in the code box and paste it into the About Me section of my MySpace profile (See Figure 9.8; you can get to your About Me section by clicking on the "Edit Profile" link on the homepage of your MySpace profile). Once you've pasted in the code, you'll want to save the changes to be able to view the page. Sometimes when you preview your profile while editing, it won't actually look like the final product. Figure 9.9 is the final product of my Bloom layout.

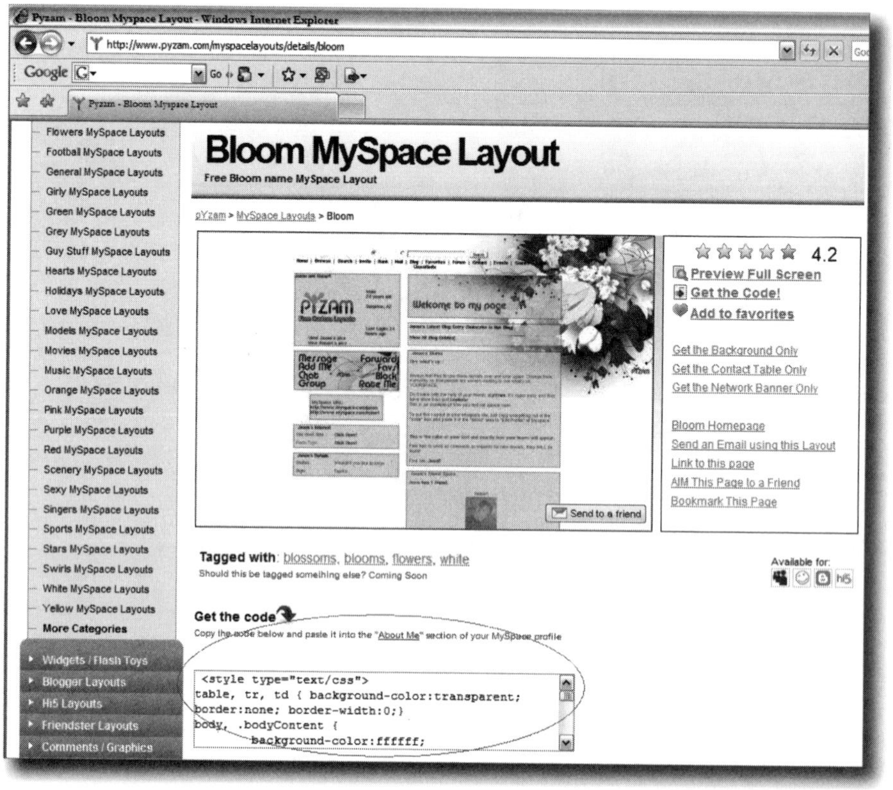

FIGURE 9.7.
Retrieving codes for MySpace templates.

FIGURE 9.7.
Retrieving codes for MySpace templates.

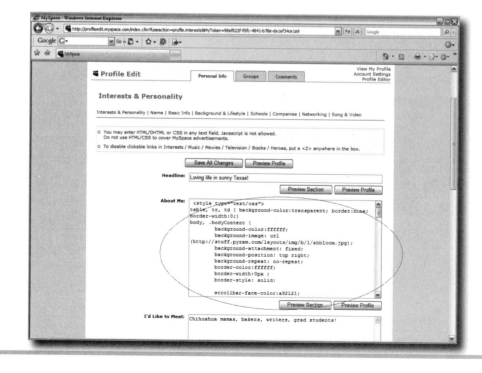

FIGURE 9.8.
Pasting a template code into your MySpace profile.

FIGURE 9.9. A new MySpace layout using a predesigned template.

Sometimes the layout may not turn out quite like you expect. For instance, often there will be extra lines separating the About Me heading on your profile from the text you actually type in. Because it looks pretty silly to have a big gap in between the heading and what you've written, now's the time to use your HTML skills to do some tweaking. Go back to the "Edit Profile" link and take a look at the code you've pasted into your About Me section. If there are a bunch of <br> before the text you've typed in about yourself, try deleting them—we already know those tags cause a line break. You can tweak all sorts of things by using what you know about HTML. For instance, if you don't want the text you type in be bold, then try removing the <b> tags (don't forget to remove the final </b> tag as well), or if you'd like your text to be italic, add an <i> tag.

Once you've tweaked the layout to your liking, you'll probably want to add other custom features to your MySpace as well. This is where you'll want to look into MySpace generators. MySpace generators are programs you can find on various Web sites that will generate code for custom MySpace features. For instance, say you want your Top 8 to actually be your Top 20, or you'd like to have your own "online now" icon that's more exciting than the boring blinking orange guy. One of my favorite sites for generators is MySpace Geeks (http://www.myspacegeeks.com). This site has many different profile tweaks and widgets. For example, you can get code to hide your Top Friends box entirely, center your entire profile, or resize the images in your comments so that they don't stretch out your whole page. Usually these sites will generate the code for you and then tell you where you need to paste it in your profile. Play around with different things, but always remember a few principles of good design, and don't fall into the trap of "hideous and annoying" profile pages!

Principles of Good Design

Here are some things to keep in mind when developing and designing your MySpace page:

1. Don't make your background so busy or colorful that it distracts from your text boxes, or makes your site difficult to read. This is the most common MySpace "newbie" mistake! A visitor to your page should never have to strain to read your text boxes. You can still have a colorful, graphic background, but make sure that your text boxes have a solid background color. Figure 9.10 is a good example of a graphic background with readable text boxes.

FIGURE 9.10.
A MySpace layout combining graphics with solid text boxes.

2. Make sure there is plenty of contrast between the text on your page and the color of your text boxes. For example, don't use white text on a light blue background. And, be careful about translucent backgrounds in text boxes; sometimes you can start to see the background image of your page bleeding through the text box, making your text more difficult to read.

3. Try to make sure the elements on your profile line up with each other, and that your boxes are roughly the same size and shape. Also remember that it's pretty annoying for most people to have to scroll a long ways out to the side of your profile to see everything, so try not to make your profile too wide. If you have a widescreen monitor, your profile might not look stretched out to you, but it could to other people with smaller screens. Ask a friend with a smaller monitor how it looks on his or her screen.

4. Check to make sure all of the links on your profile are working correctly, especially if you have made your own custom contact table. Sometimes if the code for a contact table gets messed up, you can click on the "Message Me" link but it won't actually take your visitors to a page where they can message you. It's always a good idea to check your links!

5. Don't overdo it. That sounds simple enough, right? Limit your applications to the things you really love, because putting a bunch of extraneous stuff on your page will make the loading time a lot longer and become very distracting for people who visit your page. Don't flood your page with 18 different slideshows or a bunch of giant blinky graphics.

Here's a short list of sites I love to find MySpace layouts, generators, and cool graphics you can post in your friends' comments sections. Like any Web site you go to, don't download anything to your computer unless you're certain it's from a trusted source.

→ http://www.pyzam.com

→ http://www.myspacegeeks.com

→ http://zwani.com

- → http://def-layouts.com

- → http://msnerdslayouts.com

- → http://www.kawaiitown.com

Facebook

Facebook, often abbreviated "fcbk" on the Internet, is a SNS created in 2004 by a Harvard University student (Phillips, 2007). In the beginning, Facebook was only open to other Harvard students. Eventually it opened to other university students, then high school students, and now everyone. That's great news, because Facebook is one of the hottest SNS's out there (the second-most popular, next to MySpace). It also has some of the most advanced privacy controls, which makes it a site both you *and* your parents can appreciate.

Facebook has some unique characteristics that are a little bit different from MySpace. For starters, it's grouped around networks—people you know through your school, your employer, or your hometown. When you join a certain network, you're connected with other members of that network. That makes Facebook a great place to search for classmates and people from your hometown. You won't always be able to view a person's profile, even if he is in your network; it all depends on how that person has set his privacy controls. You can always message a person though, or send her a friend request—making friends on Facebook is incredibly easy! Once you are friends with someone, you can view his or her profile and exchange "wall" messages (short public posts that pop up on your profile page).

To get started with Facebook, the first thing you'll want to do is create your profile. At the top of your homepage is a menu bar that will always be on the top of Facebook pages—click "edit" next to the "Profile" link. Then you'll want to start filling in all of the fun stuff about yourself. There are sections where you can talk about your interests, your hobbies, your favorite movies and TV shows, your favorite music, and your favorite quotes. You'll also probably want to upload a picture of yourself to be the default picture on your page (Facebook calls this a profile picture). You can add as much information as you'd like to your profile, but as soon as you're done, save your changes and click on the "Privacy" link on the right side of the main menu bar at the top of your screen.

Facebook privacy controls are very complex and customizable. If you want to put information such as your cell phone number on your Facebook profile, make certain in your privacy controls that this is viewable *only* to your friends—people you know. Never disclose your phone number or address to people other than your real-life friends, not even people who might be in your school or employment networks. Your phone number, address, and e-mail address can be controlled under the "Contact Information" tab. It's also a good idea to limit the visibility of your e-mail address to just your friends, unless you want to end up with a whole bunch of spam later on.

There are a few important privacy pointers to remember on Facebook. The first is that your profile by default is visible to all of your friends and everyone in every network you belong to. So, if you join your high school's network, you need to make sure that everything you put on your profile is appropriate for everyone at school to see—even the teachers! If you don't want everyone in your high school network to be able to see your profile, then you will need to change the very first category on the Privacy page, "Profile." You can set it so that all of your networks, some of your networks, or only your friends can see your profile. For instance, I belong to three networks—Ithaca College, Texas State University, and Austin, TX—and only my friends and people in these three networks can see my profile (see Figure 9.11).

FIGURE 9.11.
Setting privacy controls on Facebook.

You also can see in this picture that my Basic Info, Personal Info, and Status Updates are viewable only by my friends and school networks, not by the Austin, TX network. Videos and photos with me in them are only viewable by my friends. Same thing goes for my wall, which is where my friends leave comments for me. Remember that your friends could post embarrassing pictures of you and link the pictures to your profile by "tagging" them, so use care when you decide who can see photos and videos with you in them. It's always better to be safe rather than sorry later on. When you're done creating your profile, click on the Profile link at the top left of your screen and view your profile to make sure everything looks the way you want it. It will look something like Figure 9.12.

FIGURE 9.12. A sample Facebook page.

One of the first things you will want to do on Facebook is find your friends that are already using Facebook. Click on the little triangle next to the "Friends" tab at the top of your screen to see a drop-down menu of several choices. You'll want to go all the way down to the "Find friends"

option, then decide how you'd like to import your contacts. You can find people that you e-mail or chat with in different IM programs, or you can simply search for people by name. If you've already joined a network or two, you can find people in those networks as well. Once you start finding your friends, you'll send them a friend request, which they'll need to approve.

When you log onto Facebook, your homepage will display one giant "News Feed," or information on what all of your friends are doing on Facebook. Your News Feed will tell you if a friend updated her status, changed her profile picture, added pictures to an album, became Facebook friends with someone else, accepted an invitation to an event, added an application to her profile, and much more. The News Feed can even display what of your friends wrote on another friend's wall! That makes keeping track of your friends really easy on Facebook.

Unlike MySpace, Facebook does not allow its users to change the HTML on their profile pages—so you can't add the kind of custom look to Facebook that you can with MySpace. But like MySpace, Facebook has a ton of great applications that you can add to your profile to really reflect your personality. You can show off the music you listen to, the movies you've seen lately, or the books you love. You can play games like Scrabble, join a Vampire army, make a profile page for your dog, or even help fight global warming with a virtual garden! Of course, you also can share links, post pictures, and link to funny YouTube videos. To check out just how many applications there are (more are added every day), type something that interests you into the "Search" box located at the lefthand side of your screen. Try something simple, like "music." At the top of your results list you'll see a tab on the very right called "Applications," which will tell you how many applications

> ### (i) Check This Out
>
> Is there something you wish your Facebook page could include? Anyone can develop applications for Facebook, which provides an open platform for users to create applications available to all Facebook users. If you're interested, it will take some advanced knowledge of coding and Web hosting beyond the scope of this book. However, if you go to the very bottom of your Facebook page, you can click on a link called "Developers." On the next page, click on the "How to Build an App" link under the Get Started menu. This page will provide you with the details you need to get started making your own Facebook applications.

Facebook found dealing with just music (right now there are more than 300!). You can search for all kinds of applications this way.

Facebook groups are another cool feature. You can join thousands of Facebook groups with people who share common hobbies, interests, or beliefs. Just type a keyword into the same search box you used to find applications (try "music" again) and then click on the results tab that says "Groups." There are more than 500 groups that have something to do with music, so you might want to narrow your search results a bit! Try searching for your favorite band, TV show, or movie, then join a related group to show the world that you're a true fan. Remember that the names of the groups you join are displayed on your News Feed, as well as your profile page.

Three of Facebook's most popular features are usually displayed on people's profiles: notes, posted items, and photos. Photo albums work in the same basic way as the albums on MySpace. Underneath the search box on the top left of your screen, you'll see a link called "Photos." Click that link and you'll see all of your friends' recently updated photo albums, as well as options to create your own albums and upload photos to them. Your two most recently updated photo albums will appear on your profile page by default.

Notes and posted items are somewhat unique to Facebook. Notes are simply messages that you post on your profile for everyone who has permission to see your page. A lot of times, notes are announcements to your friends—I recently wrote a note to let all of my friends know at once that I was going to my hometown to visit for a few days. You can tag your friends when you post a note, so they'll receive a notification that they should read your note. Posted items is another very popular feature that happens to be exactly what it sounds like—you can post links to other Web pages, videos, and pictures, all neatly organized in a small box on your profile behind simple text links. Items that you post will often show up in your friends' News Feeds, so remember that this is a very public feature.

In the past 4 years Facebook has grown incredibly fast, and teens all over the world are helping to decide its features and contribute to its future. A lot of people have both MySpace and Facebook profiles—there's no reason to have to choose just one!

Flickr

Flickr isn't a SNS in the strictest sense of the word, but it definitely includes elements of an SNS. Flickr was designed specifically as a photo sharing community—a site where you can upload and organize your photos, plus connect with other Flickr members. As Flickr has grown, it's started to add more and more SNS-like features that go beyond simple photo uploading. But at its heart, Flickr is first and foremost a site where you can store, organize, and share your photos.

Photos that you upload on Flickr become a part of your Photostream, a visual history of the things you upload to Flickr. As you upload photos, you can designate the level of privacy that each photo has. For instance, you can make your photos viewable by everyone, people you've designated as family, people you've designated as friends, or only yourself. On a free account, your Photostream will always display the most recent 200 photos that you've uploaded. You can delete pictures from your Photostream, but once you delete them they're removed from Flickr forever.

A lot of the basic things you'll need to get started on Flickr are listed under the tab called "You" on the menu bar at the top of your screen (see Figure 9.13). Click on the "Upload Photos and Videos" link, and Flickr will walk you through a process to upload your photos. Once you've selected a photo from your computer and uploaded it, you'll be able to give it a title,

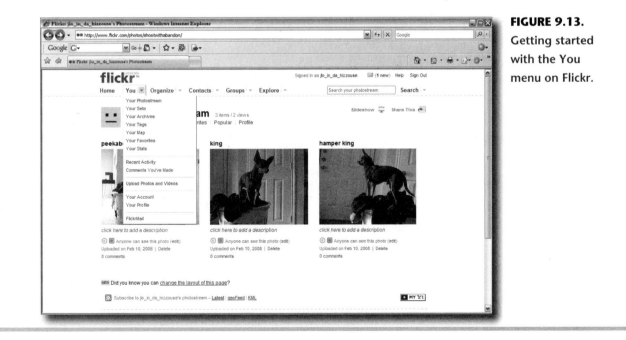

FIGURE 9.13.
Getting started with the You menu on Flickr.

a description, tags (whatever label or keyword you'd like to tag the photo with—for instance, "Chihuahua" if you've uploaded a picture of your dog), or add the picture to a set. A set is basically just a bunch of photos that you group together. You also can create groups of sets, called *collections*. You'll find all of the options to organize your photos under the "Organize" tab on the main menu bar at the top of the screen.

One of the first things you'll want to do on Flickr is look under the "You" tab and head to the Your Account page. Your Account is where you can update your personal information and set your privacy and permissions. For example, if you don't want people to be able to download your photos, you can set an option to disable downloading. You also can control who can comment on your photos, who can see the notes you write about a photo, who can share your photos with others on Flickr, and other similar functions.

Once you've got some photos uploaded, the real fun begins. Click on the "Groups" tab at the top of your page and try searching for a keyword of your choosing. I'll pick "Chihuahua." Immediately, more than 600 groups pop up! Find a group that you think you'd like to join, then click "Join" to become a member of that group and add photos to the group pool; this also allows you to add to the group discussion (see Figure 9.14). Joining groups is great way to make friends with people on Flickr who share your interests, but don't forget that you can also add contacts by importing friends and family from your e-mail and chat programs, just like MySpace and Facebook. You'll find that feature under the "People Search" option in the "Contacts" tab at the top of your page. Just click on the link that says "use your address books."

One of the best ways to find fun content on Flickr is to simply head over to the Explore Page, which is listed—as you might guess—under the "Explore" tab at the top of your screen. The Explore page contains content that the employees at Flickr find interesting—interesting photos, sets of photos, groups, and other unique content. Whenever you're looking to waste some time on Flickr, the Explore page is a good place to start!

One of the most popular uses of Flickr is to host photos for people's blogs. Blogs have gotten increasingly popular over the past few years, and more people are putting photos and other media into their blogs to make them more interesting than just plain text. Because many blogging

FIGURE 9.14.
A sample Flickr group homepage.

sites don't have dedicated space for users to upload their photos, sites like Flickr are teaming up with blogging sites to help you make your blog more dynamic, exactly what we're going to talk about in the next chapter— which is all about blogging!

Summary

In this chapter, we discussed how to join and create profiles on a number of SNS platforms. You even learned how to utilize your HTML knowledge in combination with templates to personalize your MySpace page and tricks for getting the most out of other social networking sites. Once you feel comfortable networking on the Web, you should check out the next chapter on building your Web presence through blogging.

☞ Challenge Questions

→ Using what you've learned about html in this book, take a prede-signed template (or the basic MySpace template) and modify it. What further lessons on html do you need to learn to truly make it unique?

→ Open the privacy controls on Facebook and walk your parents through a demonstration of how Facebook allows you to set your privacy so that only certain persons can see different aspects of your profile. Which sections of your profile would your parents like you to keep private? Was it easy or difficult to choose your privacy settings?

→ Pick 10 of your favorite photos for a photo experiment. Upload the photos into at least two of the following sites: MySpace, Facebook, or Flickr. Save the albums with the same name each time and make sure to label each of your pictures. Which site is the easiest process for creating albums? Which allows you to personalize your albums the most?

10

Spilling Your Guts:

Blogging and the Creation of Weblogs

What Is a Blog?

BLOG is short for "Weblog," or a Web site where one person or a group of people write regular entries about a certain topic. The first blog was probably started back in 1994, when a college student named Justin Hall began publishing a list of links to sites he'd visited (Wortham, 2007). The term *weblog* didn't actually pop up until sometime around 1997 and was jokingly shortened to just "blog" in 1999 ("It's the links," 2006). In 1998, the first blogging sites began to appear—first Open Diary, then Livejournal in 1999, shortly followed by DiaryLand and Blogger. In 1994, there were only a handful of blogs on the Web; by December 2007, Technorati.com, a blog search engine, was tracking more than 112 million blogs! (Technorati, 2008)

Today, blogs usually are much more than just links to other sites. Sometimes blogs are personal journals or diaries; sometimes they have a specific

> **This chapter will:**
>
> → tell you exactly what a blog is,
>
> → help you find templates to build your blog, and
>
> → provide tips for you to promote your blog and gain readers.

topic (like music or cooking); and sometimes they aren't even exactly text—art blogs, photo blogs, and video blogs have gotten popular in recent years. Blogging is fast, easy, and cheap, so if you feel like you have something to show or tell the world, then a blog is one of the best ways to do it.

Most blogs have a few unique features. The first is that the entries are listed in reverse-chronological order, so that your most recent entries are always at the top of the page. This means your readers won't have to scroll or hunt to find your new entries. Makes sense, right? Another important feature is commenting—usually, readers of your blog can comment on the entries. Of course, a lot of blogging sites will let you disable commenting, but comments are part of what makes a blog, a blog. In some ways, blogs can work like SNS's—your friends can leave comments for you a lot like the "wall" or commenting space on a SNS.

ⓘ **Did You Know?**

Researchers have tried to analyze how blogs become popular and how one can judge a blog to be read frequently enough to qualify it as a popular site. They have studied both blogrolls and permalinks to come to the conclusion that permalinks can boost popularity more quickly than blogrolls, in part because permalinks to your blog denote that others are reading your blog and deem it valuable enough to post a link to it elsewhere (Wikipedia, n.d.).

Another fairly common feature of blogs is a blog roll. Blog rolls are just a list of links to other blogs you recommend reading, usually set off to the side of your own blog. Having a blog roll makes your blog visible to more people, because when you link to other blogs, those bloggers will sometimes link back to you. Having a blog roll also can let your visitors know that you have a certain type of blog, or that you associate with certain types of bloggers.

There are a couple of other important terms to know that deal with blogs. A *permalink* is the Web address (URL) of any particular, single blog entry. So, even though your blog homepage has a bunch of your entries listed with the most recent at the top, each entry has its own page where it exists permanently and can be easily found—without having to scroll through dozens of blog entries. When you want to send a particular blog entry to a friend, make sure you send the permalink and not your blog's homepage. Depending on the number of entries, scrolling through a blog homepage can take forever! The permalink also is usually the place where you'll find the comments for that blog entry, if there are any.

Another term you might need to know is *blogosphere*, or the entire community of blogs on the Web. This term was coined by a blogger in 1999 as a joke (Graham, 1999), but the word eventually stuck and came into popular use. It has taken on new meaning as blogs have exploded in popularity. These days, some blogs have gotten so influential that you'll even hear journalists on TV talking about "news from the blogosphere." The blogosphere often is considered a measure of public opinion—a way to find out what's popular or interesting to the public. There actually are Web sites that track how fast and how far information (like popular sites, news stories, or YouTube videos) travels through the blogosphere. Something that gets reposted on blog after blog can spread to a huge amount of readers incredibly quickly, especially when you consider that some popular blogs have more readers than some large newspapers!

Examples of Teen Blogs

More and more teens are starting up blogs for a variety of different reasons. Some of them want to show off a hobby of theirs, like drawing or photography. Some of them want a personal journal for their thoughts about school or life. Some of them want to inform people about a particular topic, like technology issues that might interest teens.

The following sections provide examples of a few teen blogs that we happen to like.

Biscuit Rat: http://www.biscuitrat.com

Biscuitrat.com is the blog of an 18-year-old Texan named Ranjani who attends the University of Texas. Much of Ranjani's blog deals with her personal life, but she also writes about blogging platforms and Web

FIGURE 10.1.

Biscuitrat.com design.

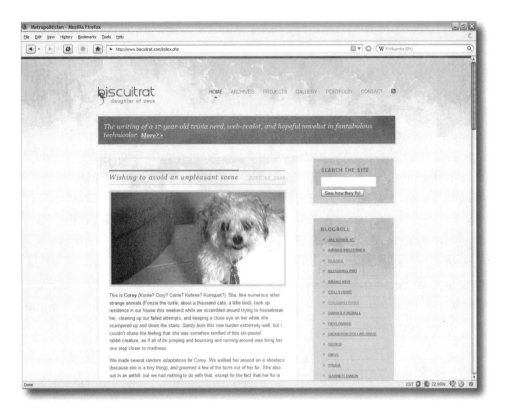

design (one of her many hobbies), offers commentary on social and political issues, and shares bits of the stories she is always writing.

Take a look at the design of Ranjani's blog in Figure 10.1. It's clean and simple, with a blog roll on the righthand side of the page and a handy search box right above that. Ranjani has also put a main menu bar at the top of her homepage, so her visitors can navigate her page easily. Click on the link at the top called "Portfolio" (see Figure 10.2), and you can check out the cool Web design projects that Ranjani has been working on lately!

Lylium: http://lylium.org

Lylium.org is the blog of 19-year-old Erin, a photographer and student in Oregon (see Figure 10.3). Besides being a place where Erin can talk about her life, her blog showcases some of her fantastic photography and is a good example of a photo blog combined with a traditional text blog. One of the neat things about Erin's blog is her method of organization—all of

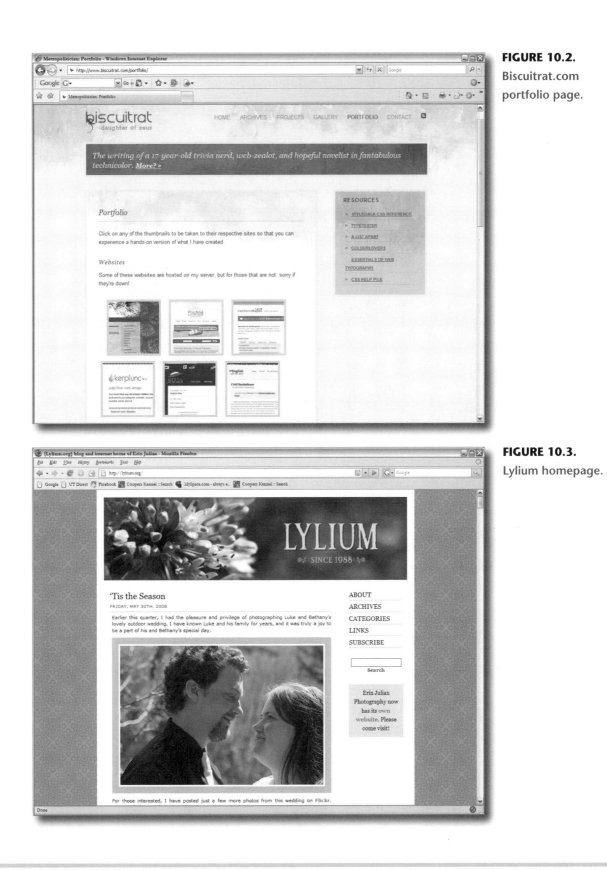

FIGURE 10.2.
Biscuitrat.com
portfolio page.

FIGURE 10.3.
Lylium homepage.

her entries are put into different categories, which you can see by clicking the "Categories" link on the righthand side of the page. Coming up with creative ways to categorize or tag your blog entries can really add to the appeal and readability of your blog!

Teen Hot Spot Blog: http://www.courier-journal.com/blogs/hotspot/blog.html

The "Teen Hot Spot blog" is published by *The Courier-Journal*, a traditional newspaper in Louisville, KY (see Figure 10.4). The Hot Spot is an interesting example of how sometimes traditional media outlets like TV and newspapers collide with blogs. It's also interesting because it's written by an entire group of teens, about 17 in all. The entries have all kinds of topics, from flying the Confederate flag, to voting in the next presidential election, to making it through your senior year of high school. All of the entries are written by teens with teens in mind, and it's really cool to see how the many different voices blend in just one blog. Check this one out if you'd like to get a feel for a group-written blog.

FIGURE 10.4.
Teen Hot Spot homepage.

You could potentially start a blog to show off your sketches, support a political candidate, talk about American Idol, or just write about your life—there's no limit to what you can do with blogs. But now that you're excited to get started, you need to know which blogging site will best fit your needs.

Blogging Sites

There are a number of blogging sites on the Web, but some are easier to use than others. The easiest sites will let you pick your blog's main theme from predesigned templates and do most of the technical work for you—while still allowing you to customize the look and feel of your journal. Some of these sites include Blogger.com (Google's blogging platform), Xanga, and LiveJournal.

Blogger

Blogger.com was launched in 1999, making it one of the earlier blogging sites on the Web (Blogger.com, 2008). Blogger is easy to use and a good choice for those who use other Google services or have a Gmail account, as your Gmail account can serve as your Blogger login. If you use the Google Toolbar, there even is a Toolbar feature called "BlogThis!" that allows anyone with a Blogger account to instantly post a link of the site they're on straight to their blog. Blogger has group blogging capability, so more than one person can contribute to a blog. Blogger also lets you edit the design templates that they give you—you can easily change the fonts and text colors. If you're handy with HTML, you also can design your own Blogger templates, or you can look for sites that have predesigned Blogger templates. Pyzam.com has Blogger layouts, as well as MySpace layouts, and there are plenty of other sites that specialize in Blogger layouts. If you know how, Blogger also lets you use their service to host a blog on your own domain. So, if you've already purchased http://www.yourname.

com, you can set up your blog on that address as opposed to the standard default Blogger address (which would be something like http://yourname. blogspot.com).

If you decide to use Blogger, you'll register for an account and then pick a name for your blog. Once you're up and running, you'll want to get used to the Blogger dashboard. The dashboard basically is your Blogger homepage and the starting point for managing your blog. From your dashboard you can view your blog (or blogs, if you have several on Blogger), create new posts, edit your old posts, and change the settings or layout of your page. You also can view and edit your profile, which is linked to your blog. The dashboard contains Blogger's own corporate blog, "Blogger Buzz," so you can stay up-to-date on the recent happenings on Blogger (see Figure 10.5). Last but not least, your dashboard contains many helpful resources—even video tutorials—to help you do things on Blogger.

FIGURE 10.5.
The Blogger Buzz feature.

Once you've got your blog looking like you want it, try adding a post by clicking on the "New Post" link at the top of your dashboard. You'll end up on a page that's basically a big text box and functions a lot like any word processor, such as Microsoft Word. You can type in your content or copy and paste from a different document, change your font or typeface, add a link or a bulleted list, or import pictures and video. Click on the button that looks like a picture—it's called "Add Image"—and you'll see how easy it is to add a picture or graphic to your blog. You can either upload one right from your computer, or you can paste in the URL of a photo you've got hosted on a different site, such as Flickr. Once you've added a few entries, your blog will start to look something like the recipe blog in Figure 10.6, except, of course, designed by you.

FIGURE 10.6. A sample blog with multiple entries.

LiveJournal

If you'd like to have a blogging site that really focuses on communities and making connections with other bloggers, then LiveJournal might be the site for you. LiveJournal was launched in 1999 and as of May 2008, has more than 15 million blogs (appropriately called journals) on its site

(LiveJournal, 2007). The majority of LiveJournal's users are in the 15–24 age range, and about ⅔ of them are female, so it's an especially good place for girls to feel at home (LiveJournal, 2008).

LiveJournal has always focused on connections between its members. One of the most interesting things about LiveJournal is that, kind of like a SNS, it allows you to create a friends list. Your friends are displayed on your User Info page (basically a profile). The especially cool thing is that you can give people on your friends list special permission to read the journal entries that you don't want to make public by marking an entry "friends only." You also can read all of the recent entries in your friends' journals on one page (your "friends page"), instead of having to go to several different blogs.

The other neat thing about LiveJournal is the communities. Anyone can make a community on nearly any topic, but so many of them already exist that you're bound to find a few you want to join. Communities are basically just group journals where everyone who joins the community can make regular posts to it. Often communities have a particular topic, like poker or celebrity gossip, but you could make a community for any purpose—even just to give your real-life classmates or friends a place to post messages to each other.

The look of your LiveJournal can be customized, but if you'd like to do more than pick from the options LiveJournal gives you, you'll need to search for communities that offer LiveJournal layouts. Or, you can learn LiveJournal's layout language, which is not HTML (like MySpace) but a unique language called S2. There are many communities dedicated to helping people with S2, and even more communities dedicated to making LiveJournal layouts, so whichever option you choose, a custom LiveJournal look shouldn't be too hard to achieve! Figure 10.7 is an example of a custom-designed layout community.

Xanga

Xanga is another good choice for teens looking to start a blog. It also has been around since 1999, when it began as a site to share book and

FIGURE 10.7.
LiveJournal layout options.

music reviews (Rubenking, 2003). Today, Xanga has somewhere around 40 million users worldwide, a large number of them young people.

If you decide to sign up for Xanga, the first thing you'll want to check out is your homepage, where you can add a post to your blog; import photos, video, or audio; or edit your profile. Xanga's version of communities is called "blog rings," and you can join as many blog rings as you want. It's a great way to meet people who share your interests or live in your area. You also can customize the look and feel of your journal from your homepage. Xanga accepts HTML layouts and a large number of communities exist just to design Xanga layouts (some of the most popular are http://blogring. net and http://createblog.com). If you don't want to use a custom HTML layout, you also can pick from different "skins" that Xanga offers.

Xanga has a couple of unique features. The first is "Pulse," or a personal mini-blog that you can keep on the move, updating it from your cell phone. This is a cool option if you want to let your friends know what's going on without writing a long entry. The second is Footprints—a way for you to track visitors to your site. As long as they're signed in to Xanga, you can get a list of the people who visit your blog, so you'll always have an idea of who's reading. Like other blogging sites, you can set the privacy level on all of your entries. You can friends-lock your entries so that only your friends on Xanga can view them, or you can Xanga-lock your entries so that only other Xanga users can view them. You also can block certain people from commenting or subscribing to your blog. Unlike some blogging sites, Xanga also has an instant messaging feature that allows you to chat more directly with other Xanga users.

Other Options

The three blogging sites I've described are not your only options for creating a blog, of course. Many more predesigned blog sites exist on the Web, and if you've gotten really good at html, you can always create your own. One option that might appeal to Macintosh users is iWeb, which comes built into every new Mac in the iLife program on Mac OS X. This simple program allows you to use custom templates created by Apple (so they're pretty cool designs) and just fill in your text. You can drag and drop images from your iPhoto library and change colors and fonts by clicking on the options across the top of the screen. If you have a MobileMe account through Apple (an e-mail and chat account you pay for separate from your computer), you can publish your site for free on the Web. Otherwise, you'll have to publish your site on a separate server or host such as the one offered by GoDaddy.com for a yearly fee.

Getting Readers

Regardless of what blogging site you choose, you'll need to know how to drive traffic to your blog if you plan on making your blog public. There are a few simple ways to do this. First, you will want to link your blog to your Facebook, MySpace, or other SNS profile page if you've got one. The easiest way to do this is to simply copy and paste your blog's URL into a section of your profile, such as the "My Website" field on Facebook. If you know how to use a picture as a link, you can create a badge—or a small graphic that links back to your blog. Badges are a little more interesting than text links, and they entice people into clicking. There are even a few sites that can help you create badges if you decide you'd like to have one.

Besides telling your family and friends, and joining communities or blog rings, there are some simple things you can do to directly increase traffic to your blog. The first is to get onto blog directories, like http://www.BlogCatalog.com. Blog directories are basically just big lists of blogs that people submit themselves, often categorized by topic. Think of it as a blog phone book. Having many blogs in one directory allows readers to search for blogs they might be interested in, so it increases your blog's visibility. Other blog directories you might want to check out are http://www.bloggeries.com and http://www.blogadr.com.

One of the most effective, but more advanced ways to drive traffic to your blog is to index (add) your site to a blog search engine, the most popular of which is http://www.technorati.com. Search engines like Technorati use different kinds of technology to determine the popularity of certain blogs and links in the blogosphere, by tracking how many people link to and comment on different blogs. The most popular blogs often are displayed on Technorati's homepage, which is designed to give you a snapshot of what's popular and relevant in the blogosphere at the moment. If you are interested in adding your site to Technorati's search engine, you'll want to visit

> ### ⓘ Did You Know?
> Technorati, a popular blog tracking site, gets its name from a blending of two words—technological and literati—referring to the technological version of intellectuals.

http://www.technorati.com and read their FAQ's to get an idea of how Technorati works. Other popular blog search engines include Google Blog Search (http://www.blogsearch.google.com) and Blogdigger (http://www.blogdigger.com/index.html).

One of the best ways to drive traffic to your blog is simply to read, and link to, other blogs. When you comment on other blogs, people who read those blogs may find themselves interested in your own blog. Keeping a blog roll on your page will encourage other bloggers to add you to their own blog roll, as well.

Remember that high-quality, well-organized content is what keeps readers coming back to a blog. So, write relevant, interesting posts and tag them with keywords or use some kind of simple organization system.

It's easy to get people to your blog, but with millions of blogs for people to choose from, it's a little more difficult to make them loyal readers. Always encourage your blog readers to subscribe to your blog, add you as a friend, or subscribe to your RSS feed if you have one. Before you know it, your blog will have a loyal following!

Summary

This chapter showed you how to find host sites for your blog. Once you set up and start writing your blog, you can use the tips in the last part of this chapter to get a good readership base built. And, be sure to check out some of the suggestions for what should and should not go on a Web site in order to protect yourself in the next chapter.

☞ Challenge Questions

➔ Once you have your blog set up, play with including links to various sites within the text of your blog. For example, if you're writing about the new movies coming out this year, link the movie names to their trailers housed on another site.

➔ Explore the various blog catalogs by choosing a few keywords or interests that you have considered blogging about (try words and phrases like "movies," "rock music," and "video games"). How can you set up your blog to be different from others on the same topic?

11

Watching Your Back:

Cybersafety

How to Stay Safe Online

This chapter will:

→ discuss the basics of cyber-safety, and

→ provide tips for staying safe online.

A LOT OF KIDS assume that you have to be pretty dumb and really unlucky to find yourself in an unsafe position online. That's just not true, and telling yourself "it won't happen to me" is the fastest way to get into trouble. Most of us know that protecting our identity online is important, but what does protecting your identity really mean? And, what else can we do to stay safe online?

If you are 15 or younger, there's a good possibility that sites like MySpace will automatically make your profile private—so that only people you approve as friends can view it. Generally, only people who know your last name or your e-mail address will be able to send you friend requests. These kinds of safeguards are for your own protection, so don't try to get around them (that could get you in big trouble with MySpace *and* your parents) and be careful of who you approve as a friend. Setting your profile to private is only effective when you're not adding strangers as friends! Believe it or not, in the summer of 2007 MySpace deleted the accounts of **29,000** registered sex offenders—29,000! And, that's certainly not including those offenders who've simply never been caught. In recent years, MySpace has actually been sued by the families of several teenage girls who were assaulted by men they met on MySpace ("MySpace deletes," 2007). When it comes right down to it, there is no such thing as "too safe" on any Web site. MySpace has a setting that allows teens to block everyone over the age of 18 from contacting them or viewing their profile. This setting is something you should consider using.

If you choose to keep a public profile, here are some things you need to know.

1. **Avoid giving out or posting any identifying information**. That especially includes your last name and address, but be careful about your phone number as well. A simple reverse phonebook search online can identify the street address associated with most home phone numbers. Some teens think that giving their cell phone number is safe, but that's not entirely true, either. And, your parents will probably have a few questions for you when they receive the phone bill! Remember that the safest way to communicate with anyone online is through e-mail or IM, but be extremely careful about the kinds of information you give out. Many SNS's allow you to join groups or networks based on your hometown or your school, which usually is fine—but combining that with other bits of information, like your class schedule or pictures of you, could be all it takes to single you out by someone who has bad intentions. As a general rule, it's a good idea to make your photo albums private, especially if you are younger than 16. Whenever you add something to your profile, just ask yourself: Would I want someone who could harm me to have this information? If the answer is no, then don't post it.

2. **Avoid meeting people from the Internet in person.** At some point or another, you may want to meet someone in person that you've talked to online. Maybe it's a cute girl from the school across town or an older boy who says he'll help you with homework. You may feel 100% certain that this meeting will be safe, but remember that the only way someone can hurt you physically is if you're in the same place. That means being 100% safe isn't possible when you meet someone in

person, especially if you want to meet them alone. Before you decide you want to meet someone face-to-face, *talk to your parents*. They may decide it's OK as long as they drop you off some place public (like a mall), meet your online friend, and pick you up at a certain time. This kind of situation is entirely up to them and even if you don't agree, you need to trust their judgment. Most parents are pretty reasonable, and they won't have a problem with you hanging out with someone your age that you met on MySpace, as long as they've met the person and know the situation. If you are absolutely set on meeting someone in person but you are *not* going to tell your parents (which is never a good idea to begin with), use common sense and *never, ever go alone*. Agree to meet some place *public*, and bring some of your friends along with you. This is the golden rule of meeting someone face-to-face. Breaking this rule can have very terrible consequences. It's not exaggerating to say that a great deal of people online are pretending to be someone they're not. One of the biggest "tricks" that offenders use online is to tell teenagers that they're in their early 20s, and then admit to being older later on—once they have your trust (DiPaolo, 2006).

3. **Don't talk about sex or other inappropriate topics with strangers.** Just don't do it—you are potentially making yourself a target. If you are receiving unwanted sexual advances, especially from someone older than you, tell your parents immediately and cease all communication with that person. Don't try to "trap" the offender or collect any "evidence." Let the authorities handle that. And, never use a Webcam with a stranger.

4. **Read between the lines.** As terrible as it sounds, most cases of teens being hurt by someone they have met online are avoidable. When you first start chatting with someone online, especially someone who seems interested in a relationship with you, you need to be able to read between the lines—to understand the things that he or she isn't telling you. If you are a 15-year-old girl being approached by a man claiming to be 25, or 32, or even 20, do you really think that man has your best interests at heart? And, not just girls are at risk—boys are prey for online predators as well. Most of the scary people online aren't anonymous ones who will figure out your identity and come abduct you when no one's looking. Most of them are ordinary-seeming people

who will try to manipulate you by being flattering or supportive. They will figure out your insecurities, because they know how hard it is to be a teenager, and they will ease your insecurities to make you feel that they care about you. They will convince you that they are your friend so that they can get something out of you. There certainly are plenty of nice people online, but always remember that some of them are only acting nice because they want something.

Working With Your Parents

One of the best ways you can guarantee a fun and safe environment online is to work with your parents. Most teens are hesitant to let their parents into their online lives, but that can cause problems when parents begin to feel shut out. Be as open with them as you can. A lot of teens seem to think that if they tell their parents about creepy people or unwanted sexual advances online, their parents will simply restrict access to the computer. You can avoid this entirely by sitting down with your parents and promising them that you will immediately tell them about anything dangerous, suspicious, or just plain creepy that happens to you online. You can promise that you'll avoid talking to strangers about anything that makes you feel uncomfortable. And, you can promise that you won't put your identity at risk. Perhaps most importantly, go over all of your privacy controls—on both Facebook and MySpace—with your parents, and let them know what you are choosing to expose online. If you let your parents know that you are aware of online dangers and you know what to do about them, they're much more likely to relax and give you a little personal space. Your parents' main concern is protecting you, and some of the things they do might seem like an overreaction. You can help keep them from overreacting by making it very clear that you're as concerned about your safety as they are. Keeping your promises to them about reporting anything dangerous is extremely important—it will keep the relationship between you and your parents healthy and stable.

Some parents may want to install software that blocks you from certain sites or chat programs. These parental control programs also may be capable of monitoring everything that you do online. In fact, these programs could be on the household computer without you even realizing it. The bottom line simply is that you need to understand that you are never "alone" and that all of your actions online can have real-life consequences. Rather than arguing or pouting, prove to your parents that you are safe and trustworthy online. You can do that simply by being as responsible as possible. It also can't hurt to give them some Web sites that deal specifically with online safety, and let them know that you've read them. Here are some good ones:

→ http://www.connectsafely.org

→ http://www.csriu.org

→ http://www.safeteens.com

→ http://www.getnetwise.org

Other Safety Concerns

Harassment and physical harm are not the only safety concerns you'll need to consider when you go online. While not as immediately dangerous, teenagers can do things online to not only damage their image but even get themselves in legal trouble. Here are a few rules that you'll definitely want to follow to keep yourself from getting into any serious trouble.

1. **Don't post anything incriminating.** We probably all have at least a few friends on MySpace or Facebook that like to brag about skipping class, post pictures of themselves with cigarettes, or write blogs about taking their mom's car somewhere without permission. Any of that is a really, really *bad* idea. It can get you in

(i) **Check This Out**

The Internet and your computer are not the only places you need to be concerned about your safety. The increase in technology also creates safety concerns for other mobile devices, like cell phones and PDAs. The Web site ConnectSafely includes a great list of tips you can use to take care of yourself on your favorite mobile devices. You also can share these with your parents to help show them that you plan to be responsible when using that great new device you've been eyeing. The tips can be found at http://www.connectsafely. org/safety-tips/safety-tips/cell-phone-safety.html.

trouble with your parents, your school, and even the police. Recently, a group of teenagers was actually suspended from their high school after one of them posted a weekend party photo of the group drinking alcohol. In other words, don't think that just because the things on your profile happen away from school or home, that your teachers or parents won't hear about it. It's very likely that they will, especially with the kind of gossip that travels around high schools and middle schools. It's also important to remember that an increasing amount of employers are looking at Facebook, MySpace, and other sites online to gather information about potential employees. So, if you're 15 or 16 and looking for your first part-time job, you definitely don't want to have anything on your profile that makes you look silly, irresponsible, or immature. Remember this rule: If you wouldn't post it on the front of your locker for all of your classmates and all of your teachers to see, then don't put it on a public profile. And, be aware that "private" profiles aren't always so private. Someone on your friends list could always show something incriminating to another friend, who might show it to someone else, who might show it to someone who doesn't like you—and then that person tells a parent or a teacher. It happens more often than you might think.

2. **Treat others how you want to be treated.** This rule applies just as much online as it does in real life. Bullying people online, which seems easy enough to do when you feel "anonymous," is going to make you a target for revenge. Not only that, but some methods of bullying are actually illegal. Not long ago a Missouri mother and her teenage daughter created a fake MySpace profile to hurt another girl (named Megan) in the daughter's class. The mother and daughter pretended to be a cute boy named Josh, and started an online relationship with Megan, only to break up with her later on. They sent her cruel messages from "Josh," including one telling her that the world would be better off without her. Not more than an hour later, Megan took her own life. The mother, who masterminded the whole hoax, was charged with the federal crimes of conspiracy and accessing protected computers without authorization ("Woman indicted," 2008). But worst of all, a young girl lost her life. It sounds like an extreme case, but this kind of bullying happens every day online, and you should never be a part of

it. It *will* backfire on you or start a confrontation at school, which can lead to further trouble. Play it safe and treat others politely and with respect. Everything you say and do online can come back to haunt you, especially if your friends become ex-friends.

3. **Be careful about what you say.** Blogs often are thought of as very personal, and for that reason people like to write about all sorts of thoughts and feelings—especially when they're angry or upset. Writing about your anger is healthy, but be aware when what you're writing might be upsetting to other people, especially if you are singling them out. Recently, more and more bloggers have gotten into legal trouble because companies or other people have accused them of defamation (the false injury of someone's good reputation or character. When defamation is in written form, it usually is called *libel*.). So if you are really mad at a guy at school, making up a story about him in your blog (or even exaggerating a "true" story) is an *extremely bad idea* that can land you in a whole pile of trouble. The same is true for companies—if you have a snotty waitress at a restaurant, and you go home and blog about how the place was overrun with rats and there was hair in your food, the company could strike back at you for false claims. Always remember that if your blog is public, then lying (or even exaggerating) about a person or a company is a quick way to get yourself in trouble. Newspapers, magazines, and TV shows have to adhere to defamation laws—your blog is in that same sphere of public media.

Summary

Staying safe online is a combination of common sense, good judgment, honesty, and simple politeness. If you make it a priority to always follow these rules (and ask your parents if there's something you're not sure about), your online experiences will be both safe and fun.

☞ Challenge Questions

→ Sit down with your parents or guardians at your computer and check out at least one of the sites on cybersafety mentioned in this chapter. Which rules would they like for you to implement as you surf the Web? Together, reach a compromise that sets up the best privacy and safety options for your computer use. Remember, *follow* those rules. It doesn't do anything for building your parents' trust in you to agree to boundaries and go way beyond them!

→ Look back at all of the projects you've created when using this book. Do you feel comfortable talking to other kids and teens (and maybe teaching others) about how to use html, build a great SNS, or write a blog? Try to share your knowledge with friends or a family member. And, most importantly, have fun!

Glossary

Application: An application (or app) is something that can run on your computer, like Microsoft Word, Internet Explorer, Photoshop, iTunes, or games like solitaire and chess. On Web sites like Facebook, apps are features that can be added to and run on your personal page to reflect your personality, like quizzes, games, and virtual programs.

Attribute: An attribute is an additional and optional piece of information added to a tag that further defines the formatting (appearance) of the Web page. For example, the < **p** > tag makes a new paragraph. Adding the align attribute < **p align** = **center** > will center the paragraph.

Blogosphere: The entire community of blogs on the Web.

Browser: A browser, or Web browser, is the application (or program) that you use to display Web pages on your computer. The browser is responsible for taking a URL, going out on the Internet, finding the site associated with the URL, sending a request for the Web page to the site, receiving HTML in return, and then interpreting the HTML to create the Web page you see. There are several different Web browsers, but Internet Explorer and

Netscape Navigator are probably the most popular for Windows, and Safari and Firefox are the ones used most often on Macintosh computers.

Desktop: The desktop is simply the screen you see on your computer after you start up. It includes the taskbar (or dock on a Mac) at the bottom and a number of icons (little pictures) for different applications and folders.

Domain name: A domain means a specific part of the Internet (determined by the IP, or Internet Protocol, address, which we won't go into here). What it means nontechnically is that part of a URL that comes after the "www." So, for Prufrock Press, the domain name is prufrock.com.

Extension: All of the information on your computer is stored in named bundles called files. Traditionally, files, especially those that hold information for an application, have a name and an extension separated by a period, like "mypaper.doc," "firstpage.html," or "shoppinglist.txt." The ".doc," ".html," and ".txt" are the file name extensions. Your computer often uses the extension to figure out which application to use to open the file (as well as which icon to use to represent the file). Typically, ".doc" indicates a Microsoft Word file, ".html" means your Web browser, and ".txt" means Microsoft Notepad or Macintosh TextEdit. You can right-click on a file icon and select "Properties" to see a file's extension. (*See also* file.)

File: As we describe under "extension," information on your computer is stored in named bundles called files, and a file usually has a name and extension. You double-click on the icon for a file to open that information. (*See also* extension, icon.)

Font: *Font* has a remarkably complicated technical meaning dating back to when books and manuscripts were printed using letters on little pieces of lead that had to be framed, lined up, and inked and then pressed onto the paper. But its approximate meaning is the kind of text used in an application, like Word or Notepad, used for creating documents. A font has a face, or typeface, like Arial or Times New Roman, that specifies how the letters look, and a size, like 12-point.

Hosting: Hosting means using a Web server to make someone's Web site visible to everyone on the Internet. There are many outfits that will host your Web site (your collection of Web pages) under your domain. It's actually possible to do this yourself on your home computer. But it really only makes sense to host your own site if your computer is on and connected to the Internet all of the time.

HTML: Hypertext Markup Language, the language used to specify how Web pages look.

HTTP: Hypertext Transfer Protocol. Once upon a time (not all that long ago, actually) when you typed a URL into your browser, you had to put "http://" before the "www" part. This would tell your browser that it should use HTTP as the language to ask for and receive the HTML for the page you wanted. There are other languages, or protocols, that run on the Internet, but HTTP is by far the most common and relevant to most people. Now most browsers automatically use HTTP if you just type in the "www . . ." part of the address. (*See also* URL.)

Hypertext: Hypertext is a word invented early in the computer era that roughly means "text with links in it." Once upon a time, before HTML was created, there were a number of different hypertext systems. Any of these would allow you to read text on your computer and click on a link in the text to go to another part of the document or another document (or file) all together. HTML pretty much dominates the hypertext systems no because it's used on the World Wide Web. (*See also* HTML.)

Icon: An icon is a little graphical image (a picture) that represents files or applications on your computer. Typically, a file with a certain extension will show up with a particular icon that makes it recognizable, so all Word documents (extension: .doc) will have the same icon. (*See also* extension.)

Image file: A file on your computer that contains an image, which is a (usually large) set of numbers that describes the color of each pixel in the image. Image files typically have ".bmp," ".gif," or ".jpg" extensions, although there are many more image formats available. Because image files tend to be large, you should be careful if you try to send images as e-mail attachments. (*See also* pixel.)

Internet: The Internet is a vast, worldwide set of computers hooked together with wires. The wires used to be regular phone lines (yes, the computers on the Internet once had to "call each other" to connect). But, now they are typically high-speed wires. The Internet is connected so that there are different ways to get from one computer to another. That way, if one way is blocked or too busy, the communication can take another route. The Internet supports e-mail and browsing, among other things. It is the basis for the World Wide Web, in sort of the same way that roads are the basis for automobile driving.

Java: Java is a powerful, general-purpose programming language. It was developed in part to run as part of a Web page, as a so-called "applet." It is used in a lot of places both on the Web and off. Java is *not* the same thing as JavaScript (*see also* JavaScript).

JavaScript: JavaScript is a computer language that is written as part of a Web page (as you'll learn in this book). Using it you can do a number of cool things. It's a real programming language.

Link: *See* hyperlink.

Permalink: A permalink is the Web address (URL) of any particular, single blog entry.

Pixel: Pixel stands for "picture element" and means a small dot that is part of a picture. Inside an image file, a pixel is one or several numbers that tells the computer what color that dot of the picture is. If the picture is 400 by 400 pixels, then in theory we need 160,000 numbers. Thus, image files are typically very big. However, some picture formats (like GIF and JPEG) compress the file to a much smaller size.

Search engine: A search engine is a Web application (that is, an application you get to by visiting a Web page). It can search the Web for information you give it. Google is our favorite search engine.

Social networking site (SNS): A Web site that allows registered users to make a public or semi-public profile (the "social" part) and link that profile to other people's profiles (the "network" part).

Tag: A tag is an HTML formatting command, the basis for creating Web pages. You can recognize tags because they are inside angle brackets < >. Usually, tags come in pairs, one to "turn on" the command and a second that starts with "/" to turn it off. There are many, many different tags (this book only scratches the surface) and many tags can have attributes. (*See also* attributes.)

URL: URL stands for universal resource locator, and it usually means the address of a Web page. You know, the old "www.whateverpageiwant.com." There's actually a bit more to a URL, but it really isn't important for this book.

Web browser: *See* browser.

Web page: A Web page is the basic display unit of the Web. This is what your Web browser shows you on your screen when you go to a Web site.

Web server: A Web server is a computer that hosts one or more Web sites. Typically, Web servers are fairly powerful computers that are (almost) always available and are connected to the Internet with high-speed connections and special software so that many people can visit the Web sites at once without the server getting bogged down.

Web site: A Web site is a collection of Web pages that is hosted by a Web server and referenced by a URL. (*See also* URL, Web server.)

World Wide Web: The World Wide Web (www) is almost the same as the Internet. But it really means the part of the Internet that uses HTTP and HTML to store and deliver Web pages. It was the invention of HTML that allowed the Internet to become the Web and really take off for all of us. (*See also* HTML, HTTP.)

References

Blogger.com. (2008). *The story of Blogger*. Retrieved from http://www.blogger.com/about

ComScore.com. (2007). *Social networking goes global*. Retrieved from http://www.comscore.com/press/release.asp?press=1555

DiPaolo, K. (2006). *Internet predators*. Retrieved from htttp://www.connectwithkids.com/tipsheet/2006/272_mar15/thisweek/060615_predators.shtml

Garfield, S. (2006). How to make 80 million friends and influence people. *The Guardian*. Retrieved from http://www.guardian.co.uk/media/2006/jun/18/digitalmedia.observerreview

Graham, B. (1999, Sep. 10). It's Peter's fault. [Msg. 2]. Message posted to http://www.bradlands.com/weblog/comments/september_10_1999

Greenspan, B. (2006). *MySpace history*. Retrieved from http://freemyspace.com/?q=node/13

Inoue, T. (2003). *Six degrees of procrastination*. Retrieved from http://www.metroactive.com/papers/metro/10.09.03/friendster-0341.html

"It's the links, stupid." (2006, Apr. 20). *The Economist*. Retrieved from http://www.economist.com/surveys/displaystory.cfm?story_id=6794172

LiveJournal. (2007). *FAQ #4*. Retrieved from http://www.livejournal.com/support/faqbrowse.bml?faqid=4

LiveJournal. (2008). *Statistics*. Retrieved from http://www.livejournal.com/stats.bml

"MySpace deletes 29,000 sex offenders." (2007, July 24). *Reuters*. Retrieved from http://www.reuters.com/article/domesticNews/idUSN2424879820070724 ?feedType=RSS&rpc=22&sp=true

Phillips, S. (2007, July 25). A brief history of Facebook. *The Guardian*. Retrieved from http://www.guardian.co.uk/technology/2007/jul/25/media. newmedia

Rubenking, N. J. (2003, Dec. 30). Xanga review. *PC Magazine*. Retrieved from http://www.pcmag.com/article2/0,1895,1400391,00.asp

Technorati.com. (2008). *About us*. Retrieved from http://technorati.com/ about

Wikipedia. (n.d.). *Blog*. Retrieved September 8, 2008, from http://en.wikipedia. org/wiki/Blog

"Woman indicted in Missouri MySpace case." (2008). Retrieved from http:// www.ctv.ca/servlet/ArticleNews/story/CTVNews/20080515/MySpace_su icide_080515/20080515?hub=SciTech

Wortham, J. (2007, Dec. 17). After 10 years of blogging, the future's brighter than ever. *Wired*. Retrieved from http://www.wired.com/entertainment/ theweb/news/2007/12/blog_anniversary

About the Authors

When **Benjamin Selfridge** was 11, he because interested in creating Web pages and did a school project on the subject. This led to a further interest in HTML, which Ben taught himself using a Web browser and Notepad. With his dad, he wrote the book *A Kid's Guide to Creating Web Pages for Home and School* when he was 13. He is now 18 years old and a student at Bard College, where he is studying mathematics, computer science, and psychology. He programs mostly in Java and C++. He also is a talented piano player and composer and an avid listener of classical, jazz, and classical and contemporary rock music. His other interests include skiing, movies, out-of-the-ordinary fiction books, and Shakespeare.

Peter Selfridge has a Ph.D. in computer science and worked at Bell Laboratories and AT&T Labs as a computer researcher for many years in the areas of artificial intelligence, robotics, software engineering, human-computer interfaces, and more. He currently works as an independent technology consultant and researcher in the Washington area. When not working, Peter enjoys being a parent to his older children, Benjamin and Lauren, as well as his two younger children, Sarah and Andrew. When time permits, he enjoys skiing, playing the acoustic guitar, and hiking.

Jennifer Osburn is a graduate student and instructional assistant at Texas State University in San Marcos, TX, where she teaches undergraduate English and film classes. She is a future technical communicator whose interests include technology, education, baking, and making sure her two chihuahuas have whatever their tiny hearts desire.